I0698323

For Future Generations

Also by R. Thomas Sultzer:

Conception of Magnificence: John Quincy Adams and the Birth of American Astronomy

Generating History: Profiles of an Early American Family

For Future Generations
John Quincy Adams and His Love for Trees and Gardens

R. Thomas Sultzer

Dedication

To Edie and her Eden

Contents

Introduction

John Quincy Adams, the sixth President of the United States, led many roles in his life. He was a lawyer, diplomat, Massachusetts state senator, United States senator, Secretary of State, President of the United States, and United States congressman. He advocated for science by being a member and president of several learned societies. He fostered the growth of astronomy in the U.S. to an extent for which he could be called the father of American astronomy. Across these, as well as many other roles, he had a great, lifelong fondness for forest and fruit trees, and the many gardens he experienced and worked throughout his life. There was always some degree of occupation with trees and gardens no matter where he was in the world, or what official occupation he was accomplishing. Most of his gardening activities took place in the town he was born, Quincy, Massachusetts, and in Washington, DC.

Adams, called JQA by family, friends, and colleagues, applied trees and gardens in many aspects of his life and his relationship with the world around him. He used them as entertainment and education when touring gardens and forests in the U.S. and across Europe. He used them for exercise by planting, pruning, and walking among them. He used them for production when harvesting their yields. He used them for research in his experiments to successfully grow various trees and plants. He used them in business when bargaining on sales of land, and for fuel when heating his homes. He used them as therapy when he was feeling low about any perceived difficulties in his life. He marked the passage of time and the meeting of milestones through plantings and growth. He used them as memory triggers, commemorations of past events, and memorializing lost loved ones. He also used them to teach, in metaphor to describe ideas, and in his politics, both for their sake and the country's.

The legacies of JQA's love of trees and gardens carry on in several respects. There are the trees still thriving, planted by his hand, at the family homestead in Quincy, which his father called Peacefield, but he more practically called The Old House. There are other trees he planted at his son Charles's house in Quincy, which his son transferred from The Old House during the periods of his great interest in raising trees. Still more trees reside at the houses of friends and colleagues which JQA contributed to beautify their residences. There are the stands of live oaks preserved in the southern U.S. which he envisioned as the supply for naval shipbuilding, construction, and nature conservation. There is also the U.S. Botanical Garden, of which JQA played a large role in establishing.

Although he stumbled and made mistakes along the way, both professionally and personally, he remained steadfast to his conviction for the preservation of trees, and the cultivation of gardens, for providing both their yields and beauty for future generations. The details behind his convictions provide greater insight into the man he was, and the future he wished to help create.

Chapter 1: Childhood Influences, 1767-1778

John Quincy Adams was born on July 11, 1767 in Quincy, Massachusetts. The family called him "Johnny," but he later developed the moniker "JQA" to distinguish him from his father, the second President of the United States, John Adams. Quincy, Massachusetts, used to be the north precinct of the town of Braintree from 1708 until being incorporated as a separate town in 1792. It is during this period that both John Adams and JQA were born. The Adams family owned two saltbox houses next door to each other, both built in the 17th century. John Adams's father, John Adams, Sr., purchased one of the houses in 1720, and his son was born there in 1735. John Adams inherited the almost identical house next door in 1761, and moved into it with his wife, Abigail Adams, in 1764. JQA was born in this house three years later, the second of their six children.

These houses, and the small farms and kitchen gardens that accompanied them, are where JQA received his first influences in the ways of gardeners. The family moved somewhat frequently between Braintree and Boston during JQA's first seven years of his childhood, due to his father's law practice that had its ups and downs. Through it all, John Adams's farm and garden were always in his mind, and his thoughts would regularly turn to them and his family to keep him grounded and calm during stressful legal and political battles. His letters to Abigail periodically expresses his longing for both his family and his land. In June of 1774, John wrote to Abigail from York, Pennsylvania, where he was working on a legal case, and made it evident of where his real thoughts were turning:

> "My Refreshment is a flight to Braintree to my Corn fields and Grass Plotts, my Gardens and Meadows. My Fancy runs about you perpetually. It is continually with you and in the Neighbourhood of you—frequently takes a Walk with you, and your little prattling, Nabby, Johnny, Charly, and Tommy. We walk all together up Penn's Hill, over the Bridge to the Plain, down to the Garden, etc."

Abigail would frequently read John's letters to the children, or have them read the letters themselves to improve their skills. The messages about John's love for his fields sunk into JQA's mind, and when John was at home, he would take JQA and the other children out to the fields to teach them farming and gardening skills.

By September of 1774, John was pulled to Philadelphia to participate in the First Continental Congress as the conflict between Great Britain and her thirteen colonies continued to heat up toward the Revolutionary War. John spent most of the next four years in the Congress, but his thoughts were no less frequently moved toward his home. Even after the war had begun, all too close to the Adams homestead, John continued to blend his care for his lands with his concern for his family's safety, as he did from Philadelphia on May 22, 1776:

> "I want to take a Walk with you in the Garden—to go over to the Common—the Plain— the Meadow. I want to take Charles in one Hand and Tom in the other, and Walk with you, Nabby on your Right Hand and John upon your left, to view the Corn Fields, the orchards, &c. Alass poor Imagination! how faintly and imperfectly do you supply the Want of original and Reality! But instead of these pleasing Scenes of domestic Life, I hope you will not be disturbed with the Alarms of War. I hope yet I fear."

Abigail was not the only correspondent who received these flights of fancy concerning John's gardens and fields. A week after his letter to Abigail, he replied to a letter from Benjamin Hichborn, a prominent Boston lawyer and friend to Adams who was concerned for his health, saying that, regarding Congress, "Indeed if a few Things were more fully accomplished, I should think it my duty to ask Leave of my Constituents to return home to my Garden." Nearly a month later, on June 24th, he wrote to William Tudor, co-founder of the *North American Review* journal and the Boston Athenaeum, one of the oldest independent libraries in the U. S., that, "When a few mighty matters are accomplished here,

I retreat like Cincinnatus, to the Plough and like Sir William Temple to his Garden; and farewell Politicks. I am weary. Some of you, younger Folk, must take your Trick and let me go to Sleep." Lucius Quinctius Cincinnatus was the 5th century BC Roman military leader who gave up power to retire and return to his farm. Sir William Temple was the English statesman who forged the 1668 Triple Alliance among England, Sweden, and the Dutch Republic against French ambitions, but whose pro-Dutch policies were undermined by King Charles II, causing Temple to return to his carefully tended garden   of wall-fruit at his home outside London. When peace returned, he served again as ambassador, only to resume his gardening when he fell out of favor once more.

In March 1777, when the war was looking at nearly its bleakest point, John wrote Abigail the most passionate and almost poetic paragraphs concerning his farm and family:

> "The Spring advances, very rapidly, and all Nature will soon be cloathed in her gayest Robes. The green Grass, which begins to shew itself, here, and there, revives in my longing Imagination my little Farm, and its dear Inhabitants. What Pleasures has not this vile War deprived me of? I want to wander, in my Meadows, to ramble over my Mountains, and to sit in Solitude, or with her who has all my Heart, by the side of the Brooks. These beautiful Scenes would contribute more to my Happiness, than the sublime ones which surround me.

As much as I converse with Sages and Heroes, they have very little of my Love or Admiration. I should prefer the Delights of a Garden to the Dominion of a World. I have nothing of Caesars Greatness in my soul. Power has not my Wishes in her Train. The Gods, by granting me Health, and Peace and Competence, the Society of my Family and Friends, the Perusal of my Books, and the Enjoyment of my Farm and Garden, would make me as happy as my Nature and State will bear."

In May, he wrote to his son Thomas Boylston Adams, saying, "Pray, when you write me a Letter, let me know how many Calves are raising, how many Ducks and Geese, and how the Garden looks. I long to take a Walk with you to see them, and the green Meadows and Pastures." Two weeks later, he again mentioned to Abigail in his next letter, "I wish I could see your Garden and little Farm." Then, in August, he wrote, "Digging in a Potato Yard upon my own Garden and living in my own Family would be to me Paradise. The next Time I come home, shall be for a long Time." This next time would not be long, but it would be a long time before he was able to stay home for any great length.

The Continental Congress was forced to move from Philadelphia to, first, Lancaster, then York, Pennsylvania, starting in September 1777, but not before John wrote to Abigail one more time about the gardens, stating, "For my own Part I never lived in my whole Life, so meanly and poorly as I do now, and yet my Constituents will growl at my Extravagance. Happy should I be indeed if I could share with you, in the Produce of your little Farm. Milk and Apples and Pork and Beef, and the Fruits of the Garden would be Luxury to me." That November, John was selected by Congress to travel to France to negotiate a treaty of support in the war, which he accepted on the 27th. He came back to Braintree, prepared for the trip, and decided to take JQA with him at the age of eleven to be his secretary and to give him a worldly experience. It would also give him a wider education in gardening. They set sail on February 17, 1778, aboard the frigate *Boston*[1].

---

[1] The *Boston* was a twenty-four gun frigate launched from Newburyport, Massachusetts in 1776. She captured a number of British ships before the British themselves captured her in 1780, and sold her in 1783.

Chapter 2: The Garden Tourist in Europe, 1778-1785, 1795-1801, 1809-1817

The first trip to Europe for John Adams and JQA was relatively brief, lasting only one month with Adams receiving no diplomatic instructions. They returned in August 1779, as the voyage home was longer than their stay. In November, the pair left for France again after Adams was appointed the minister in charge of negotiating a commercial treaty with Great Britain and ending the war. This time, Adams's son Charles joined the pair. The ship had to dock early in Spain due to a leak, which forced a six-week trip over land to reach Paris.

JQA's experiences in Europe over the next seven years, and other periods of time, were filled with touring the personal gardens of important people with whom his father worked, and the gardens of castles and estates of European kings, queens, and prime ministers. This was actually a popular pastime for natives and visitors alike, evidence of which is shown in a letter from Abigail Adams to JQA in 1786, while JQA was in college and Abigail was in France; "Viewing the Houses and Gardens of Noblemen, constitutes one of the principle Summer amusements of this Country, Natives as well as strangers, and the Gardens of all the Nobility are open to the Latter." The first three years of JQA's time in Europe were spent primarily in and around Paris, France, and The Hague, Holland. JQA also began his life-long diary during this period, encouraged in it by his father. The first entry about gardens came in December 1779, during the overland trip from Spain to France, specifically from Ferrol to A Coruña in Spain, with his father and ten others:

> "The ground is in General well cultivated. Corn, Turnips, and all other vegetables stand in the Ground. In the Month of December the Ground is cover'd all about with a sweet verdure and all appears like the Month of May."

This almost poetic passage was written by a twelve year old, which shows his intelligence beyond his years. By August of 1780, JQA was well settled in The Hague, Holland, and was charmed by what he saw, evidence of which is in his diary entry of August 7, 1780:

> "This beautiful place lies in the Centre of a great number of fine cities and Villages, with which it has an easy communication by Canals, on the Sides of which a thousand agreable Objects perpetually rise up, that make the journies on them seem too short. For wherever the Passenger turns his Eyes, he sees either beautiful Country-Houses magnificent Gardens, fine Meadows, or charming villages. And indeed,

go which way one will, one always finds delightful Paths, or Walks paved with Bricks, and Shaded with Several Rows of Trees; so that the Neighbourhood of the Hague exhibits, on all Sides of it, whatever can form a fine Landscape."

The first garden tour which he wrote about in his diary on August 9, 1780, was what he called the Physick Garden in Leiden, Holland, which is now known as the Hortus Botanicus, or Botanical Garden, formed by Leiden University in 1590. It is now the oldest botanical garden in the Netherlands. JQA also saw here the tomb of Charles de l'Escluse, a French botanist who contributed to the establishment of modern botany. He was best known by the Latin version of his name, Carolus Clusius. He developed new cultivated plants, such as the tulip, potato, and chestnut, from other parts of the world. From 1573 to 1587 he was the director of the Holy Roman Emperor's garden in Vienna, and spent the later years of his life teaching in Leiden, where his cultivation of tulips in the botanic garden was the beginning of the Dutch tulip bulb industry.

Two weeks later, on August 20th, JQA toured the gardens at the county seat of Daniel Crommelin, a New Yorker who moved to Amsterdam in 1724 to be his father Charles's primary European contact of his company, The Holland Trading Company. Owner of the Amsterdam mercantile house Crommelin & Zonnen (originally in partnership beginning in 1737), Crommelin supported American independence and with whom, as the elder Adams's Diary records, John Adams had early and frequent contact. Over these six months, JQA took additional tours of the Hortus Botanicus.

In July 1781, John Adams's secretary, Francis Dana, was selected to become the U. S. Minister to Russia. JQA's father decided that it would be a great experience for him to accompany Dana to St. Petersburg as his secretary. On the 7th of July, JQA made the three-hour trip to the city of Utrecht in order to meet up with Dana and prepare for the journey east. JQA was sure to make note in his diary of the country seats with their gardens owned by citizens of Amsterdam lining the road for seven to eight miles out of the city. At fourteen years of age, JQA set out across Europe with Dana to have more wide ranging experiences, including new gardens to tour. He kept records of the scenery he saw along the way, especially including the forests and the condition of the soil.

Once JQA arrived in St. Petersburg, his primary port of call in support of Francis Dana was Peterhof, a series of palaces and gardens in St. Petersburg commissioned by Tsar Peter the Great in the early 1700s. The primary garden of Peterhof then and now is the Jardin d'ete, or the Summer Garden, on the banks of the Neva River. JQA's first tour of the Summer Garden was on May 15, 1782, but throughout the period of June through September of that year, he took many walks through the garden either alone or with various companions, reporting at least twenty-three occurrences. He also accompanied Dana and others on June 23, 1782, for a tour of the Jardin de Narischkin, the garden at the seat of Alexis Narischkin, chamberlain, diplomat, and scholar serving Tsarina Catherine the Great. A visit to this garden was a popular Sunday pastime of the "higher classes" in St. Petersburg.

Once his time as Francis Dana's secretary was complete, JQA traveled on his own back west across northern Europe, spending time in a number of countries before reuniting with his parents in Auteil, France, in the summer of 1783. While there, JQA toured the gardens at the Domaine de Chantilly, the seat of the Bourbon family in Chantilly, France, with gardens of over 284 acres; during JQA's time, it included a French-style garden created by André Le Nôtre in the 17th century, and an Anglo-Chinese Garden created during the 18th century. Domaine de Chantilly was owned by the Prince de Condé, Louis Joseph de Bourbon (1736–1818), a strong supporter of the monarchy at the time of the French Revolution. JQA described the most interesting features in his diary:

> "The Gardens are Superb; there is a small river which runs down from above the Gardens, and furnishes all the jet d'eau's with water. There are in the Gardens several small, houses, which on the outside look like Peasants hut's, but are most elegantly furnish'd, and are beautiful inside. There is an equestrian Statue of the Connetable de Montmarenci in bronze, and a marble Statue of the grand Condé."

The next day, April 10, 1783, JQA traveled with his father and Benjamin Franklin to visit the house of Thomas Barclay, the first U. S. Consul to France, where he toured its garden, which he described as "a small and pretty one filled with fruit Trees."

John Adams became the U. S. Minister to the Netherlands in 1782, and then was appointed a second position as the U. S. Minister to the United Kingdom in April 1785. He soon had to make a trip back to France, and JQA traveled with him. On April 21, 1785, they toured the gardens at the estate of Louis de Noailles, who was the Duke of Ayen (1737-1766), the Duke of Noailles (1766-1793), a Marechal of France (1775-1793), and grandfather of Revolutionary War hero, the Marquis de Lafayette. The estate was in St. Germain en Laye, where King James II of the United Kingdom held his Court after he was driven away from England as a result of the Glorious Revolution of 1688.

JQA returned to Quincy in mid-summer 1785, but was soon enrolled at Harvard College in Cambridge, Massachusetts, earning his bachelor's degree in 1787 and his master's degree in 1790. He also studied law in Newburyport during his graduate work. This did not stop him, however, from touring local gardens. On August 22, 1785, he traveled a few miles outside Cambridge with a few classmates to the estate of a Colonel Jeremiah Wadsworth, the commissary general for the continental army during the Revolutionary War and a U.S. Congressman several years later. He showed them his fields of grain and grass, and his orchards. The following year, 1786, he toured a grape arbor in the town of Newburyport, a short distance from the Merrimac River. According to JQA it was "50 feet long and 20 wide, with 14 arches form'd with boughs of trees, in such a manner that the leaves only could be seen. A number of flowers and grape vines were entwined with them, so that clusters of grapes were hanging over our heads." The subsequent summer, 1787, he toured the gardens of William Brattle, a British loyalist during the Revolutionary War, but a Harvard alumnus who was friendly to the College until his death in 1776. His interest in horticulture aroused during his stay in England, Brattle planted his spacious grounds, which extended to the Charles River, with flowers and fruit trees and had a small pond, shaded by willows, stocked with fish. For the benefit of Harvard students he laid out a long walk bordered with trees and built a bathing house on the river, where students might learn to swim.

In 1790, after earning his Master's degree, JQA opened a law practice, renting office space in downtown Boston. He had no time for horticultural interests, and made no entries in his diary over the course of his law practice from 1790 through the first six months of 1794. On June 5, 1794, JQA received a letter from Congress in Philadelphia informing him that President George Washington appointed him as the first U.S. Ambassador to the Netherlands, which gave him his next opportunity for garden tourism. By the end of the month, JQA journeyed to Philadelphia, arriving on July 9th after being detained in Newport, Rhode Island, for four days due to foul sailing weather. While in the city, he met with President Washington, Secretary of State Thomas Jefferson, Secretary of War Henry Knox, and Secretary of Treasury Alexander Hamilton to receive instructions for his new post. By August 8th, he began his travel back to Boston, stopping in New York City and dining with General Horatio Gates, who had been in retirement since the end of the Revolutionary

War. JQA arrived in Boston on August 19th. After nearly a month   of preparations in Quincy and Boston, he set sail for England on September 17th, landing at Deale on October 14th. JQA spent several weeks in England on business before sailing across the North Sea to the Netherlands, arriving at The Hague on October 31st. While in English places including London, Deal, Dover, and Harwich, he made time during his stay to admire the "verdure of the fields, the luxuriance of the harvest, the infinite variety of delightful prospects," which "still exhibit to the admiration of the traveller scenes which almost realize the fictions of a fairy land." He was also distracted by meeting the three daughters of Joshua Johnson, England's Consul General to the U. S., and brother of Thomas Johnson, a governor of Maryland.

Once JQA was in the Netherlands, and the spring of 1795 arrived, JQA took time on May 2nd to visit the two estates of William Willink and his brother, John. William Willink was a wealthy Amsterdam merchant, and one of the investors in the Louisiana Purchase. JQA had dinner at William's country seat, named Bosch en Hoven, and took tea at John's country seat, named Bosch en Vaart. He was not greatly impressed with the houses or their gardens, writing in his diary, "They are handsome, though not magnificent houses, with gardens according to the common custom of the country. The gardens have nothing remarkably agreeable; everything is cut up and fashioned by the rule and square. The hot-houses appear to be the most useful part. We saw strawberries in their state of full maturity; apricots half ripe, and peaches of the size of a walnut. The wall-fruit trees are covered every night during the season with double mats of reeds and flags." More regularly, JQA took walks in the woods near his lodgings in Amsterdam. Also, in June 1797, he joined a small party of travelers to visit the little towns of Saardam and Broek, in the North Holland portion of the Netherlands. He noted that each house had a small yard or garden encircled by a fence.

In the midst of his appointment in the Netherlands, JQA traveled back to England for the exchange of ratifications   of the Jay Treaty, which settled outstanding issues following the Revolutionary War, and did business with Joshua Johnson, spending the winter of 1795-96 and part of the spring there after arriving on November 10th. On December 6th, he witnessed three of Johnson's seven daughters playing music and singing, as was a regular occurrence at the household. However, on the day after Christmas, December 26, 1795, he once again heard an evening concert from the daughters, considering them all "pretty and agreeable," but noticed "the middle daughter singing prettily." After this event, he began spending nearly every evening at the Johnsons's, both for business and for courting Louisa Catherine, Johnson's illegitimate middle daughter. JQA again noticed how prettily Louisa sang on February 7, 1796, and accepted Louisa's friendship ring on March 2nd. He did not return to the Netherlands until the end of May.

Even through his diligence in daily diary entries, he very seldom recorded his interactions with, and feelings for, Louisa. After another year in the Netherlands, with regular correspondence between JQA and Louisa, he went back to

England on July 11, 1797. The purpose for his return was clear when he mentioned wedding planning on July 21st, and married Louisa on July 26, 1797, at All-Hallows-By-The-Tower Anglican Church in London. Louisa would eventually be the first foreign born First Lady in U.S. history.

Throughout most of his father's presidency, 1797 to 1801, JQA transitioned to being the U.S. Ambassador to Prussia, which included portions of modern day Germany, Austria, Hungary, and Poland. During his travels throughout the country, he noticed pine forests; cultivated fields of wheat, rye, oats, barley, buckwheat, tobacco, cabbages, and potatoes; and went out on picnics in local gardens with the nobility   of the time. Louisa was always at his side. He also visited a few of the major gardens in Prussia, including the following:

- The gardens of Sanssouci in Potsdam, Germany, the summer palace of King Frederick the Great, who reigned 1740-1786.
- The gardens of Dresden Castle in Dresden, Germany, the primary palace of King Augustus II (The Strong) who reigned 1694-1733.
- The Teplice Botanical Garden, which surrounds the House of Clary-und-Aldringen, major royal families of Prussia, now part of the Czech Republic. He toured the garden with Count Yurii Alexandrovich Golovkin, the Russian Minister to Stuttgart.
- The Saxon Garden, a public garden in central Warsaw, Poland, founded in the late 17th century and opened to the public in 1727. The Saxon Palace, Brühl Palace,

The Great Salon, The Blue Palace, the Church of St. Anthony of Padua, and the Iron Gate were here during JQA's visit, but, later, were either partially or completely destroyed during World War II and the Communist takeover.

When his tenure was finished, JQA returned to the United States in September of 1801. However, he had one more chance to tour European gardens ahead of him. In 1809, JQA was appointed as the U. S. Ambassador to Russia, and traveled to St. Petersburg for a five-year stay. He resumed his regular walks in the Summer Garden. In 1810, he revisited the Jardin de Narischkin. In addition, he visited the following gardens:

- The Stroganov Garden at Stroganov Palace in St. Petersburg, built for Baron Sergei Stroganov in 1754.
- The garden of the Institute of Ways and Means School of Engineers in St. Petersburg.
- The gardens of the Oranienbaum, a royal residence located on the Gulf of Finland, west of St. Petersburg, built for Aleksandr Danilovich Menshikov, Peter the Great's right-hand man between 1710 and 1727.
- The gardens at the St. Petersburg home of the Italian Duke de Serra Capriola, spacious and beautifully laid out, and covered with forest-trees planted by the Duke more than 20 years before JQA's visit.
- The palace and gardens in Czarskozelo in St. Petersburg, one of Peter the Great's other residences.

In 1814, on his trip back west across Europe, after being appointed as the lead negotiator for the Treaty of Ghent, ending the War of 1812, he made more time to visit palace gardens and made observations in a few countries where he stayed for a significant amount of time:

- Catherinendal on Lake Mörtsjön south of Reval (now called Tallinn), Estonia, built by Peter the Great of Russia for Empress Catherine, where JQA commented on the extensive gardens laid out in the fashionable style of that time.
- On the road from Antwerp to Ghent, Belgium, he observed elms, lime-trees, and poplars, with a younger growth of oaks along both sides of the road.
- La Grange, the home of the Marquis de Lafayette, outside of Paris, where the Marquis, now a General, had surrounded the house with poplars, willows, pines, firs, and locusts, with horse chestnuts and oaks at a further distance.
- Traveling from Paris to Rouen, he observed orchards in full bloom.

JQA also had one more assignment while in Europe as the U. S. Ambassador to the United Kingdom, where he stayed from 1815 to 1817, but did not take advantage of the time there to do any more garden tourism activities.

Chapter 3: A Lawyer and a Senator, 1801-1809

JQA returned to Quincy on September 21, 1801, after finishing his assignment as the U.S. Ambassador to Prussia. The family had previously landed in Baltimore, but JQA parted with his family, who traveled to Washington to stay with Louisa's family. While on his way to Quincy, JQA spent some time in New York City. He was not alone, being accompanied by his sister and brother-in-law, Abigail (Nabby) and Colonel William Smith. While there, on September 14th, they visited the Mount Vernon Garden, which is now the New York Botanical Garden in The Bronx, and the Town Hall Garden, which no longer exists, the building being razed in 1812 for construction of the current New York City Hall.

After arriving in Quincy, JQA walked with his father through the elder's farm, where JQA noticed that it had been greatly altered and improved since he had last visited it in 1794. But a few weeks later, on October 14th, he was on the road again to Washington, DC, to reunite with his wife and children, and bring them home to Quincy. He arrived at the house of Catherine Johnson, Louisa's mother, on October 21st.   The route back to Massachusetts, beginning on November 4th, took them to Frederick to visit other Johnson family members, primarily Louisa's uncle, Thomas Johnson, former first elected Governor of Maryland and Supreme Court Justice, who lived in Rose Hill Manor[2] with his daughter Ann and her family.   While there, JQA made sure to tour Johnson's garden, where Johnson taught him how to graft fruit trees and gave him a few slips of pear trees to take with him.   Due to both Louisa and son Charles Francis contracting illnesses, they spent an extra week in Frederick, and suffered through a very slow trip back to Quincy, arriving there on November 25th, the day before Thanksgiving.

Most of December was spent moving into a house on Hanover Street in Boston, which JQA had purchased on October 1st.   He was determined to open a law practice, leasing an office on State Street the day after Christmas. After the New Year, his thoughts expanded for the first time into science and politics.   He joined a local club, the Society to Pursue Subjects of Natural Philosophy, with ten other gentlemen, which would keep his mind active in scientific topics for years to come.   He also had his first desirous thoughts of getting involved in politics, but resisted those thoughts, since he felt that most politicians were men of their party, while he would be a man of his whole country.   It did not take long before his thoughts got the better of him, when

---

[2] Rose Hill Manor was built in 1792 by Thomas Johnson's daughter and son-in-law. Johnson lived with them for the last 25 years of his life after his wife died. The house is now owned by Frederick County as part of Rose Hill Manor Park & Children's Museum.

he was elected to the Massachusetts State Senate on April 1, 1802. He would not even spend a full year in this office, however.

After a busy year at his law practice and the state senate, events began happening rapidly for JQA in 1803. In February, the Massachusetts Senate chose JQA to represent the state in the U. S. Senate. By April, financial tragedy struck when the Adams's brokerage firm in England, Bird, Savage and Bird, went bankrupt, forcing JQA and his father to sell off numerous properties in which they had speculated. By June, JQA gave up his law office, since it was a very hot summer, the State Supreme Court was in recess, and he would have little legal work until needing to begin his Senate career. On September 1st, he sold the family's house on Hanover Street, and by the end of the month, JQA moved his family into the house of his birth in Quincy. These activities brought his father and him back into financial solvency, somewhat at the same place they were before the brokerage crisis began.

September was also eventful for JQA in a botanical way. This month appears to be the time of his life when he began his life-long infatuation with gardens and trees. He was a member of the Boston Academy of Arts and Sciences, and was encouraged by a few members to begin studying the *Flora Batava*, a journal on botany which they had sent to him. The journal was one of the most long-lived on the subject at that time, founded in 1800 by the Dutch botanist, Jan Kops. JQA also visited his father's fruit and kitchen garden several times, letting the elder Adams borrow his book, *A Treatise on the Management of Fruit Trees* (1803), by

Scottish botanist William Forsyth. There is evidence that he also began his first tree plantings at his house, focusing on peach tree stones.

By October 1ˢᵗ, JQA packed up his family for the journey to Washington, DC, to begin his Senate career. They arrived on October 20ᵗʰ to stay at the house of Walter Hellen, Jr., Louisa's first cousin, and brother-in-law through marriages to two of Louisa's sisters; first wife Ann "Nancy" Johnson, and second wife Adelaide Johnson. The house was on K Street, three blocks from the Capitol. JQA's first term as a senator lasted until April 2, 1804, when he set out for Quincy, arriving there on April 14ᵗʰ. Louisa and the children stayed in Washington for the summer.

A few days after returning to Quincy, on April 18ᵗʰ, JQA purchased apple trees and went to the Mount Wollaston farm the next day, settling on a place to lay out his first orchard. He had a total of 102 trees set out in this orchard, which began his passionate pastime of raising trees that would last for the next forty years. For the summer of 1804, JQA would spend at least half an hour in his garden, most days caring for his fruit trees, pruning, budding, and plastering injured trees, following the instructions in Forsyth's treatise. He was able to observe the growth of peach stones he had planted the previous September. He would also periodically check on his orchard, which in July he found "almost all the apple trees and peach trees I had planted there in the spring alive and thrifty." There was, however, a gradual attack on the peach trees by slug worms, which drove him to study the writings   of William Dandridge Peck, the first Harvard professor   of natural history, titled *Natural History of the Slugworm* (1799). He tried inoculating the trees against the slug worm, which he learned from the book, but his experiments failed. During that spring and early part of the summer, JQA was also attending the Court of Common Pleas and Sessions several times a week. He did some hunting as well, what he called "Walking out with my gun."

JQA continued to help with his father's garden and trees, and visited several friends' and neighbors' gardens, including publisher Thomas Greenleaf, Captain Benjamin Beale, and Dr. John Warren, nephew of Revolutionary War General Joseph Warren. At Warren's garden, he observed a variety of peaches, nectarines, plums, pears, nuts, and cherries. In September, he added cherry trees to his orchard. But in October, he observed the damage from a hurricane that had torn through the area, seeing over one hundred trees ripped up by the roots, and having the roof of one of his barns torn off. By that time, the growing season had ended, and JQA traveled back to Washington to rejoin his family and the Senate between October 16th and 24th. Overall, JQA did not have a very positive outlook on his first botanical efforts, writing in his diary:

> "I gave some attention to agricultural pursuits, but I soon found they lost their relish, and that they never would repay the labor they require. They require my studies, were assiduous, and seldom interrupted. I meant to give them such a direction, as should be useful in its tendency, yet on looking back and comparing the time consumed with the

knowledge acquired, I have no occasion to take pride in the result of my application."

He brought his family with him back to Quincy in 1805, arriving there on April 5th, after a few days delay in Philadelphia after his son, John Adams II, contracted chicken pox. A few days later, he purchased twenty more apple trees and had them set out in his orchard. He noted that his father went to Boston on April 13th to attend a meeting of the Agricultural Society, concerning the establishment of a botanical garden and a professorship of natural history at Harvard University. He also began his first nursery for planting seeds, stones, and acorns, raising young trees for future transplanting around his property. In addition, he laid out a garden for growing vegetables and flowers at his birth house, in which he slept for the first time in twenty-five years on April 25th. JQA's botanical activities grew into a more serious venture during the spring, summer, and fall of 1805.

During this time, JQA's focus was on fruit trees. Besides the apple trees he set out in his orchard, he set out peach, pear, cherry, and nectarine trees which had grown from the previous two years. He also planted peach, cherry, and plum stones, in addition to a few walnut acorns, in his nursery, and noticed these types of trees sprouting from stones he had planted the previous two years. In addition to his own plantings, he helped his father transfer trees at Peacefield, and examined flowers in the gardens and during his walks about both properties. He also purchased additional farmland and wooded lots which would play a role in his future botanical endeavors.

JQA actively sought botanical knowledge during this period of time through reading the popular books on the subject. Beginning on May 13th, he reading Swiss philosopher, composer, and botanist Jean-Jacques Rousseau's *Letters on the Elements of Botany* (1787), translated by English botanist Thomas Martyn. He kept up this reading, especially in June and into July, finishing on the 10th of the month. On a few occasions, he recruited Louisa and sister-in-law Eliza as an audience for his aloud reading of the letters. They also accompanied him on walks during July, which he called "botanizing," amounting to admiring and gathering flowers in the local area. A significant part of his reading time was also taken up by reading, translating, and learning Greek, and analyzing the rhetoric of philosopher Aristotle. One other activity that contributed to his education was attending Society for the Study of Natural History meetings which turned to the subject of botany.

By November 11th, the family packed up and made their journey back to Washington for the next Senate term. JQA returned alone to Massachusetts on May 3, 1806. His family stayed in Washington. This year, however, he took lodgings in Cambridge instead of his Quincy house. He had been appointed the Professor of Oratory and Rhetoric at Harvard University, and living in Cambridge was most convenient for that position.

On May 17th, he transplanted thirty-five peach seedlings, surrounding one of his brother Thomas' trees, to his nursery. By June 1st, however, when inspecting his nursery and orchard, he found nearly all of the trees he had transplanted eaten by insects, but the stones and acorns he had planted were sprouting. He combined his growing interest in astronomy with his gardening interests by gathering with the members of the Society to observe a total solar eclipse in the garden of Benjamin Bussey, a Boston merchant, farmer, and horticulturist.

Just two weeks later, however, on June 30th, he received a letter from his wife, Louisa, with the sad news that their most recently born son was stillborn, and Louisa had nearly died during her labor. Fortunately, she was recovered, but this greatly impacted all of JQA's interests for the remainder of his time in Cambridge. Louisa became healthy enough to travel by July, and arrived with the children on August 10th, after JQA had moved to a room in Boston to await their arrival. They moved to the Quincy house again the next day.

JQA eventually began visiting his gardens by late August, primarily budding and pruning his young fruit trees. On August 29th, he brought a few Brownbury pear and Magdalen peach buds from Dr. Warren's for grafting in his nursery. By late September, he wrote about the first of the trees bearing fruit, along with nuts from the walnuts, and acorns from a few oaks. He also observed walnuts growing in his father's garden that JQA had planted there two years previously. He speculated that the growth period of walnuts was from May to July, while the apple, pear, and plum grew twice in the summer, the peach all summer through, and the cherry until the beginning of September. These results and speculations inspired him once again to increase his labors in the garden. His family also made their way back to Quincy.

On October 18th, after spending time with his son, he was inspired to write of his feelings about the land and his place in it:

> "This afternoon I took George with me over part of the farm with the view to familiarize him at this season of his life with the scenes upon which my own earliest recollection dwells – I feel an attachment to these places more powerful than to any other spot on Earth, precisely because they are associated with the first impressions of which the traces remain upon my mind – These attachments are connected with some of the sentiments and opinions which I most cherish, and which I should wish my children to possess."

By November 17th, he had moved his family into a rented house on Poplar Street in Boston for the winter, and traveled back to Washington alone again. When he arrived back in Boston the next spring, on March 18, 1807, he found that the family had moved into a house which he had previously purchased on the corner of Nassau Street and Frog Lane. He also moved in for the summer. The house was on Boston Common, and he was able to witness in April that the Common "has assumed its first verdure." JQA's Harvard lectures and his return to the business of a lawyer almost entirely diminished his work in the garden, nursery, and orchard. The only activity he recorded was the transplanting of young nectarine trees in May, while regrettably noticing that both his and his father's growth of the last three years had been almost entirely rooted up, most likely by tenant farmers who had not paid attention to what they were plowing.

JQA managed to find time for educational pursuits by attending two lectures at Harvard immediately following his rhetoric lectures by Dr. Benjamin Waterhouse on plant growth and Swedish botanist Carl Linnaeus' system of botany. Waterhouse was the co-founder of Harvard Medical School, and the first physician to test the smallpox vaccine. JQA was also able to converse with François André Michaux, the son of French botanist André Michaux, who was posthumously publishing a few of his father's manuscripts. That evening, the particular subject was the younger Michaux's collecting of materials to supplement his father's work on the oaks of Carolina.

At this point, JQA's life became much too full to dedicate any more time to his trees and flowers. His son, Charles Francis, was born on September 13, 1807, and a month later, he and Louisa were back in Washington, having left the children in the care of JQA's parents. Although he was not able to physically satisfy his botanical pursuits, his thoughts regularly turned to them. An example of this occurred on November 3rd at the President's House (now the White House) when he commented on President Thomas Jefferson's and Secretary of State James Madison's farming skills – Jefferson had claimed an extreme fondness for agriculture, but no knowledge, while naming Madison as the greatest farmer in the world. JQA commented on Jefferson being delightful company, and concluded the evening as very satisfying,

The family returned to Boston in May 1808, but less than a month later, due to local political intrigue, JQA was not re-elected to his Senate seat. He continued as a Harvard Professor and lawyer, but stayed in Boston into the winter. In January 1809, he was called up to argue a legal case in the Supreme Court, spending the remaining time in Washington until the end of March. It was the case of *Fletcher v. Peck*, 10 U.S. (6 Cranch) 87 (1810), which was a landmark United States Supreme Court decision, in which the Court first ruled a state law (Georgia) unconstitutional. In July, JQA found in the *National Intelligencer* newspaper that President James Madison had appointed him, and the Senate had confirmed him, to be the Minister Plenipotentiary to the Court of St. Petersburg in Russia. As a result, he resigned his professorship in July. On August 5th, he set out for Russia on the ship *Horace* with Louisa, son Charles, Louisa's sister Catherine Johnson, nephew/secretary William Steuben Smith, chambermaid Martha Godfrey, and black servant Nelson. They arrived in St. Petersburg on October 23, 1809.

For Future Generations

Chapter 4: Secretary of State, 1817-1825

JQA returned from his years in Russia, Belgium, and England as a diplomat on August 6, 1817. After some time in New York, the family returned home to Quincy on August 18th. President James Monroe had appointed JQA as his Secretary of State in March. After conducting business and reuniting with friends and family not seen in eight years, JQA, Louisa and the children set out for Washington in this next phase of his political career, arriving there on September 20th. The family moved into a house that JQA had purchased at 244 F Street, where they lived for the rest of their Washington, DC lives, more than thirty years. The house's address is now the address of the Georgetown University Law School.

During these eight years, whether in Washington or Quincy, JQA found virtually no time to work in his garden, nursery, or orchard. That did not mean that trees and gardens were not on his mind and in his activities. In May 1818, he received a shipment of goods for the household from various locations, which included two boxes of garden seeds from Baltimore and London. After a busy first season of diplomacy, the Adamses made their first return to Quincy from late August to late September. On September 21ˢᵗ, while in Salem, Massachusetts, for a few days, JQA, with several others, visited the house of William Bentley, Unitarian minister, scholar, and early member of the American Antiquarian Society. While there, he viewed drawings from nature, including flowers, drawn by Bentley's adopted daughter.

JQA and family began their trip back to Washington in October 1818. During an early leg of the trip from Worcester to Northampton, Massachusetts, JQA observed the countryside and saw that a "Great part of it is covered with wood—Oak, Birch, and Chestnut. The cleared land apparently not fertile; generally pasturage, with some poor, thin looking Indian Corn." Arriving at Newburgh, New York, JQA, Louisa, and family stayed in a hotel owned by John Peter De Wint, a manufacturer and investor, and their nephew by marriage to their niece Caroline Amelia Smith. He convinced the travelers to spend a few days touring the Hudson River valley centered on Fishkill, New York, the location of De Wint's home, Cedar Grove[3]. They took a day to tour the mountains around West Point, nine miles from Fishkill. JQA became almost poetic in describing the views from the mountains and the river, which he wrote, "give the country a picturesque appearance of wild grandeur." On the way back to Fishkill, the wonder of his surroundings showed through his diary entry of October 7, 1818:

---

[3] Cedar Grove was built around 1814, but burned to the ground in 1857.

"About five in the afternoon we embarked again in our Sloop, and returned with a beautiful, mild and calm Evening to Fish-kill landing. We saw the purple tint of the Sunbeams lingering on the tops of the Mountains, and heard by Moon-light the distant echo of the horns blown from a boat upon the river in the passage between them."

The Adamses spent one more full day in Fishkill touring local mountains and dining with the family before setting off once again down the Hudson to New York, and eventually reaching Washington on October 14th.

On March 12, 1819, JQA had his first opportunity to support a botanist down on his luck. Dr. William Barton, a naval surgeon, medical botanist, and author, came to JQA's office seeking support in reestablishing the importance of his position at the Medical Marine Support Office in Philadelphia, or at least gaining respite from his position being determined as useless by the Secretary of the Navy Richard Thompson. Barton said that he received short notice, and would not be able to support his family. After JQA spoke with Thompson a week later, he allowed Barton three months to look about him for an alternate position before closing out his position. This grace period facilitated by JQA must have allowed Barton the time he needed to make other plans. He eventually became the commander of the Naval Hospital Norfolk, Virginia, and the first head of the Bureau of Medicine and Surgery, now the Navy Surgeon General. He also served as a professor of botany at the University of

Pennsylvania, and the dean   of the Jefferson Medical College.

In late April 1819, JQA walked across the fields to the woods north of Washington, DC, gathered some of the first flowers of spring, and noticed that the oaks and elms were putting forth their first leaves of the season. Beginning in June 1819, JQA began receiving information on trees that would occupy him for years to come in his political life, and would be a major vehicle in applying his caring for trees and the future of the United States. James Leander Cathcart, a Revolutionary War midshipmen, diplomat, and U. S. Navy agent for the protection of timber in Louisiana and Alabama, came to JQA's office and provided his most recent survey finding live oaks in those regions. This survey led Cathcart to discover that current maps and descriptions were extremely inaccurate. The preservation and use of southern live oaks for naval shipbuilding would become one of the most important issues of JQA's presidency, which would begin in 1825. Upon his return to Washington in November 1819, he discussed the import of the Chinese tick-tree with President Monroe and William Crawford, Secretary of Treasury. They likely were referring to the teak tree. Crawford believed it could be grown successfully in Louisiana, but nothing ever came of it.

That fall of 1819, JQA's father, John Adams, transferred the deeds to several plots of land to his son, which included Penn's Hill Orchard (17 acres), Atherton's Pasture (16 acres), and a smaller piece of land known as Rocky Run. Penn's Hill had wooded lots of primarily cedar and hemlock. He inspected his acquired land on October 4th, spending five hours among the woods and pastures that expanded the total area of his Quincy farm. JQA marked trees to remember the boundaries of his lots, and noticed "twelve trees, cedar and hemlock, each from 30 to 40 feet long, which had been cut down, and drawn together after the gale of September 1816, and have been lying there ever since." He tasked local workers to bring them to the farm when sledding was possible in winter to use as timber for building a barn.

JQA was quiet on the subject of trees and gardens through most of 1820, until late that December when he made his first diary entry concerning the Columbian Institute for the Promotion of Science, a learned society of influential Washington, DC, gentlemen formed in 1816. He had been a member for three years, but was attending a society meeting for the first time. The members placed JQA on a committee to petition the U.S. Congress for funds to benefit the work of the society. The following February 1821, the committee narrowed the primary purpose of the funds for the laying out and cultivation of a botanical garden. Beyond this activity, nothing further progressed, and JQA eventually traveled back to Quincy for the summer.

The only noteworthy botanical activity during the summer of 1821 came in September, and was focused on touring and observing woodlands and trees. On a trip to Princeton, New Jersey, with Louisa, his father, and others, JQA observed how advantageous it was to view the Massachusetts landscape from travel along the turnpike roads. He observed that "Pastures, Indian corn and potatoe fields, and apple orchards constitute the chief cultivation;

interspersed with Oak, walnut, Ches[t]nut and Pine woodlands." A few days later during this trip, JQA, his family and father, observed the countryside from the peak of Mount Wachusett, the highest point in Massachusetts at 2,000 feet, 60 miles from Boston. He could see the Blue Hills near Boston and into New Hampshire from this vantage point. He also observed that the largest trees on the mountain were oak, ash, and pine, growing about two-thirds up the mountain, the rest being shrubs. He also noted that "the line of separation between the large and small wood goes round the hill at the same elevation, as regularly as though it were drawn with compasses." Toward the end of the month, he inspected his Mount Wollaston farm with brother Thomas Boylston Adams, and gave the tenant farmer directions to lay out a new orchard of trees.

In November 1821, once JQA returned to Washington, continuing his duties as Secretary of State, he got back involved in botanical activities. On November 6th, Dr. William Thornton, Columbian Institute member and designer of the U. S. Capitol, visited JQA at his office and showed him his plan for the botanical garden. JQA thought it looked good on paper, at least. Over the coming months, he also continued discussions on southern live oaks, possible planting of imported tropical trees, and other forests. After his 1822 trip back to Quincy, he was elected President of the Columbian Institute, which he accepted on October 4, 1822, and remained in this position until he was inaugurated the sixth President of the United States in March 1825, having been re-elected to the position on Christmas Day of 1824. During this time, the society's botanical garden was built.

JQA eventually had discussions on planting trees in the garden.

During these last few years of his position as the chief American diplomat, JQA was able to spend some time as a garden tourist again, as he did in Europe. On September 23, 1823, JQA toured the gardens of Nathaniel Amory, a resident of Watertown, Massachusetts, with John Kirkland, the President of Harvard University. Upon his return to Washington, during November and December, he had several discussions with William Elliot of the U.S. Patent Office and Columbian Institute member, regarding the plans for the institute's botanical garden, the planting of trees being a specific topic.

On August 2, 1824, he traveled to Alexandria, DC, with Louisa, son John, and several others to visit a garden of exotic plants maintained by William Yeates, a Quaker horticulturalist who also had a tree nursery on his lands. JQA may have learned a few tips from Yeates. On October 1, 1824, in Bordentown, New Jersey, he visited the extensive gardens and grounds at Point Breeze[4], home of Joseph Bonaparte, the older brother of Napoleon Bonaparte and former King of Naples and Spain. Two days later, a few miles outside Philadelphia, JQA visited the home, Belmont Mansion[5], of federal district judge Richard Peters, who

---

[4] Bonaparte built Point Breeze in 1820 after his original house burned down. He lived there until 1839, when he returned to Europe. Point Breeze had several other owners before it was added to the National Register of Historic Places in 1977.

showed him a Spanish chestnut tree planted by George Washington just before his retirement from the U.S. Presidency. It would only be six months before JQA himself would take the oath of office as the sixth President.

---

[5] Belmont Mansion was built in 1745 by Richard Peters' father, William an English lawyer and land management agent, and was added to the Philadelphia Register of Historic Places in 1956.

Chapter 5: Presidential Gardening, 1825-1829

JQA became President on March 4, 1825. He used his office and the White House grounds as instruments to forward his interests in, and the country's stance on, trees and gardens. For the first year, however, he was too busy being the President to make any progress. One opportunity presented itself to JQA early on which he did not take. On May 24, 1825, he received a private letter from J. S. Skinner, Corresponding Secretary of the Maryland Agricultural Society, inviting him and the heads of the Executive Branch Departments to attend the next annual cattle-show and exhibition of household manufactures, at a tavern four miles out of Baltimore. After consideration, he concluded that he would become "an article of exhibition" across the country like the cattle and other objects on exhibit, and therefore declined the invitation.

During the fall and winter of that first year in office, JQA at least found time to observe the rising of the sun on various days, and how that rising aligned with landmark trees in the immediate area. These included the line of poplar trees that led away from the White House, the tall poplars that stood north and south of the Treasury Department building, and an unspecified but tall tree at the southeast corner of the State Department building.

During the latter part of June 1826, JQA had several discussions concerning trees, and maintained them as a point of interest to observe during his walks around Washington. In July, his activities toward the topic became more physically exertive, as he began to collect twigs of trees, particularly oaks, and compare them with the plates in French botanist François André Michaux's book *North American Sylva* (1810-1813). By July 5, 1826, JQA's schedule allowed him to begin thinking once again about horticulture. It was on this day that he first proposed developing a tree nursery on the grounds of the White House the following autumn. His inspiration was the passing, and his signing, of a bill by the House   of Representatives to promote planting of live oaks and white oaks, primarily for shipbuilding and other construction. With his nursery plan, beginning with the planting of acorns, hickory-nuts, and chestnuts, he still felt that he would be planting more for the country than for himself. He collected oak leaves as well from three kinds of oaks, and received artistic support from Louisa and Elizabeth, who created drawings of trees from which he could not reach the leaves.

July 5th was also one day after his father, second President John Adams, had passed away in Quincy. JQA did not find out for several days after his father's death. In the days prior to his learning of this sad news, he managed to make more observations of shellbark and pignut hickories, as well as at least five different oaks – white, post, red, black, and pin. He then traveled to Quincy for his father's funeral and management of his papers, properties, and final business transactions. This would postpone the White House nursery for more than a year.   However, while in Philadelphia, on July 10, 1826, JQA made contact with Richard Peters once again, and asked him to obtain a few acorns from the chestnut trees that George Washington and Peters' father had planted near Philadelphia.   Peters promised to provide both acorns and young trees already growing.

JQA stayed in Quincy for the rest of the summer and half of the autumn, returning to Washington in late October. While in Quincy going through his father's papers, he found a *Catalogue of the Plants and Trees in Prince's Nursery* at Flushing on Long Island, New York, which encouraged his thoughts of trees and gardens for the rest of his stay there, even in the midst of his duties settling his father's estate. He visited the estate of Thomas Greenleaf, a Boston publisher who published key documents supporting the ratification of the U. S. Constitution.   There, he perused Greenleaf's orchard, filled with sycamores, buttonwoods, poplar, birch, dogwoods, sugar maples, walnuts, and white pines.   That same day, July 18, 1826, he noted upon arriving back at Peacefield the presence of two althea trees on either side of the eastern most door   of the house. They were blooming, and many blossoms were opening.   These two trees would give him many years   of enjoyment. They were planted by his mother.   On various walks and horseback rides, he collected leaves, twigs, nuts and acorns of various trees on the Adams family Mount Wollaston farm, at the beach where he would take regular swims, and in the local woodlands. He also read Michaux's *North American Sylva*, a book with illustrations of American trees and shrubs, and two books by physician and botanist Dr. Jacob Bigelow; *American Medical Botany* (1817) and his *Florula Bostoniensis* (1814), or plants of Boston. JQA's son George Washington Adams literally borrowed the books from Dr. Bigelow himself and brought them to his father for reading. One July 23rd, he asked a neighbor, Judge Rufus Davis to bring him some acorns from his English oaks. Davis provided them on August 12th, but JQA was somewhat dissatisfied with their age, being about three years old.

Beginning on August 21st, JQA oversaw the surveying of his father's lands, the business of which continued into early October. Included in these lots were a salt marsh, woodland lots named "Joy," "Furnace," "Quincy, Beale & Savile," "Adams," and "Borlands;" a beach lot called "Gull Island;" and the "Cherry Tree Lot," named for the large tree that formerly stood out on the lot. The woodland lots became the most adventurous, sending JQA and his company through tangled forests and swamps, startling the local wildlife, and running into several rattlesnakes along the way. JQA took time, however, to study the trees, finding numerous types   of oaks (white, post, red, black, pin, Spanish), white and pitch pine, red cedar, hemlock, chestnut, black beach, basswood, shellbark and pignut hickory, black birch, yellow ash, sassafras, witch-hazel, sycamore, buttonwood, American poplar, dogwood, white birch, and maples. By September

19th, the surveys were complete, along with the sale of a few saltmarsh and woodland lots.

On October 6th, after settling the sales of land and rental of his father's farm, JQA left for what he thought was the last time, of which he was very mistaken. A few days later, on October 9th, he rode with son George to the ponds at Sterling, Massachusetts, where at least two dozen ponds of various sizes existed in the vicinity of the town. There, he observed the woods filled with oak, walnut, chestnut, maple, white pine, and birch trees, with none of very large size. He also gathered handfuls of chestnuts, with a plan to plant some in Washington, while giving a portion to George for planting in Quincy.

JQA traveled back to Washington during the latter part of October. On November 1st, he began his first plantings in the White House garden, which included chestnuts from those he received from Richard Peters from trees planted by George Washington, the ones he gathered at the ponds in Sterling, and others he had collected while in Princeton, New Jersey. He also planted walnuts and shellbarks picked from a tree in Quincy that he had planted himself in 1804. Two days later, although it would not be developed for another year, JQA spoke with the Capitol arborist, John Foy, about the tree nursery he conceptualized during the summer. He also asked Foy to select several spots to plant nuts and acorns that would not have to be transplanted later. These spots ended up within the future boundaries of the nursery, where JQA planted more Washington chestnuts, Quincy walnuts, Pennsylvania walnuts, black and pin oaks found while riding with his son John, pecan nuts, and pignuts during the remaining course of November.

JQA also proved to have developed a network of friends and colleagues who paid attention to the availability of planting materials for him, and produced results. On December 1st, fellow Massachusetts legislators, Senator Nathaniel Silsbee and Representative Benjamin Crowninshield, informed JQA that they had collected for him English acorns from the Reverend Henry Colman, a Unitarian minister in Salem, Massachusetts, and one of the most important leaders in agricultural knowledge of the time. Later in April, unfortunately, Foy informed JQA that the acorns were dead, and he could not plant them.

In 1827, JQA's activities in his White House garden and nursery kicked into high gear. Beginning on March 25th, he began observing the first signs of spring, including the greening of poplars and weeping willows, sycamores, horse chestnuts, locusts, and maples. Later, in mid-April, he began to see blossoms on the apple and peach trees. He also began reading again, this time from Scottish botanist John Claudius Loudon's *Encyclopedias of Gardening* (1826) and *Agriculture* (1825), and from French botanist Henri-Louis Duhamel Du Monceau's *Cultivation of Trees* (1755-1767) and *The Uses and Treatment of Wood* (1752). Upon consulting these books, JQA acquired conflicting feelings between the desire to dive headlong into the study of trees, and the relatively late time in his life he discovered this desire. He wrote of this conflict in his diary entry of April 24th:

"Looking into these books, I find a wide field opened before me, which I cannot expect the remnant of life allotted to me will afford me to explore, and at present the time that I can bestow upon it is so very little, and cut up with such incessant interruptions, that I fear the result of my pursuit will plunge me into inextricable confusion of mind, without contributing to any useful end."

The same day, he brought home a twig covered in white flowers which, with the help of the colored plates in Michaux's *North American Sylva* and Bigelow's *Medical Botany*, he identified as a dogwood. He had seen it at the Capitol Garden without knowing it was a dogwood.

When May came around, JQA inspected the area that would become his tree nursery, and found that two mature trees had been cut down within the boundaries of the nursery. Infuriated by this action, he called Joseph Elgar, the Commissioner of Public Buildings for Washington, to the White House, remonstrating Elgar for taking such an action before he could realize just what happening. Elgar had been working on leveling the ground, which necessitated, in his view, the cutting down of the two trees. This was part of the tasks in JQA's nursery project. His diary entry ends with Elgar's explanation, but JQA would be involved in developing and settling other disputes with Elgar over the course of his term in office.

On May 18, 1827, JQA's interests turned to the White House garden after he decided to take a walk through it and get a tour of it from the White House gardener, John Ouseley. His relationship with Ouseley would grow over the next three years, and be more pleasant and productive than his relationship with Elgar. From this first visit, he created an exhaustive list of the plants he observed in his diary. The garden and his readings occupied his time for the rest of May, and on the 30th, he began his plantations in the garden, first with red and blackheart cherry stones. The next day, he planted shelled and unshelled almonds. In June, he increased both his time in the garden, his readings, and his discussions with Ouseley. He recorded a general description of the garden in his diary on June 5th which provides the most vivid picture of how it was laid out, and what it contained:

> "Spent two hours in the garden, where, at every visit, enquiries multiply upon me. In this small garden, of less than two acres, there are forest- and fruit-trees, shrubs, hedges, esculent vegetables, kitchen and medicinal herbs, hot-house plants, flowers, and weeds, to the amount, I conjecture, of at least one thousand. One-half of them perhaps are common weeds, most of which have none but the botanical name. I ask the name of every plant I see. Ousley, the gardener, knows almost all of them by their botanical names, but the numbers to be discriminated and recognized are baffling to the memory and confounding to the judgment."

On June 6th, he found that the grounds crew, under Foy's direction and Elgar's supervision, had fenced in the area for his nursery, but it would not be fully prepared until November. His White House plantings included the following:

Pennsylvania walnuts	Quincy walnuts	hazel nuts	Peters chestnuts
apple seeds	cherries	plums	apricots
persimmons	Tulip trees	limes	catalpas
strawberries	oranges	currants	apple pippins
raspberries	mulberries	pears	gooseberries
shellbarks	shagbarks	willows	pignuts

He also transplanted shagbark, apple, walnut, and orange seedling trees into what would become his tree nursery. During this period of time, JQA also received assistance from his Belgian man Friday, Antoine Giusta, in such tasks as spading up weeds that were overgrowing the garden plants and transplanting certain trees and flowers. JQA took particular interest in Antoine's transplanting of a laurel rose, which he brought in a tub of earth, and proclaimed that he was using the Chinese method of transplanting, which he read of in a book.

During the entire month of June, and a portion of July, JQA regularly took walks in which he incorporated observations of trees, plants, and flowers, as well as collection of samples from the objects he observed. His walks took him around the Capitol Square, the fields surrounding the White House, College Hill leading up to the Capitol, the Slashes near Slash Run flowing from Rock Creek, and, of course, his almost daily walks in the garden and other areas of the White House grounds. During these walks, he plucked twigs from various oak trees; samples of wild indigo, tick-seed sunflower, and liquid amber; wild germander, cudweed, betony, and solanum; greenbrier, hawkweed, and whortleberry.

On June 19th, Foy called upon JQA to discuss the laying out of the tree nursery. JQA provided his vision for the layout, with some notions on how to develop and tend to it. He was in favor of cross-alleys with one moving in an east-west direction, and the other in a north-south direction, with a border alley around the entire nursery. He wanted the entire nursery to first be planted with grass, then replanted one section at a time with seedling trees and whatever acorns, seeds, and stones he decided upon as the work progressed. Foy left with that guidance to consider, and on the last day of June, came to JQA with three plans for laying out the fenced in nursery. JQA was in favor of a simple design with two crossing, central alleys between rows of trees, very close to his original guidance.

JQA also got into the business of preserving seeds for later planting by storing them outright or fermenting them in rum and wine. He recorded an example of these exercises on Jul 7th, listing his preservation of cherry, plum, and apricot stones, and strawberry, raspberry, currant (black and red), gooseberry, and black mulberry seeds in various ways. He did not, however, show much enthusiasm for future success in these endeavors. In the middle of the month, he observed some of these seeds under a microscope, listing the similarities and differences among blackberry, raspberry, strawberry, grape, gooseberry, and currant seeds.

JQA's reading list for the remainder of the time he spent in Washington included (the first two of which he read the most):

- Duhamel's *Cultivation of Trees, The Uses and Treatment of Wood*, and *Physique des Arbres*
- Loudon's *Encyclopedia of Gardening* and *Encyclopedia of Agriculture*
- British chemist William Nicholson's *British Encyclopedia of Arts and Sciences*
- American botanist Amos Eaton's *Manual of Botany*
- French historian Alphonse de Beauchamp's *History of Brazil*
- French botanist François André Michaux's *North American Sylva*
- American horticulturist William R. Prince's *Descriptive Catalogue of Fruit and Ornamental Trees*
- Irish-American horticulturist Bernard McMahons *The American Gardener's Calendar*
- British surgeon John Hunter's account of the Devonshire Oak in the 62nd volume of the Royal Society of London's *Philosophical Transactions*

JQA returned to Quincy in early August, but maintained his pace of planting, reading, and observing the trees and gardens around him. Not long after he arrived, on August 7th, he first dedicated a site on the property to horticultural experiments and care of the youngest trees and plants. It was a plot of land where the original owners', the Vassalls, summer house had once stood, but retained the cellar below. JQA had begun the previous autumn with plantings of oak, shagbark, and chestnuts. His regular use of what he logically called the Summer House Cellar began this August. By September 10th, he had a Quincy nursery staked and fenced off, working with Solomon Augustus Farrar, whom he had hired to tend to his gardens and trees while he was in Washington. He also created four seedling tubes to experiment with growing trees from seeds. Here, he planted the following:

limes	tamarinds	pears	plums
apples	peaches	nectarines	oaks
cherries	chestnuts	shagbarks	

He also found time to tour a few gardens that were not his own. He strolled through the grounds of Medford, the estate of Boston merchant Peter Chardon Brooks, who in two years would be his son Charles's father-in-law. He toured the garden of the President of the Massachusetts Horticultural Society, Henry Dearborn, who was also a U. S. Congressman, as well as that of Israel Thorndike, a Boston merchant and one of the earliest financiers of the Industrial Revolution later in the 19th Century. He visited the Harvard University Botanic Garden, and took walks and horseback rides through local forests to collect acorns for planting.

On October 3rd, JQA made his first major plantings in his Quincy nursery, which was formed from the northwest corner of his garden. Here he planted twenty rows English, black, white, and grey Oak acorns; peach, plum and cherry Stones; apple and pear seeds; whole peaches and Apples; horse chestnuts; and ten Pennsylvania walnuts gathered the previous year. He also had a complex discussion with multiple neighbors about their desires and his potential plans to sell portions of his lots of land for straightening roads, allowing a neighbor to build a house, and for the building of a new schoolhouse.

JQA travelled to Washington during the period of early and mid-October. During the trip, while on a stop in Baltimore on October 16th, he visited the site of the Battle of North Point, fought on September 12, 1814. He observed the thick forest trees shedding their leaves. John Barney, a U.S. Congressman from Maryland, pointed out to JQA an old oak tree that was said to have endured twenty musket balls in its bark during the battle. JQA took the opportunity to collect half a dozen white oak acorns to later plant in his White House nursery. He also went on rides through the forest with his son John to collect other acorns and nuts for planting. By November 8th, the White House nursery was prepared, and JQA made his first deliberate plantings in it the next day with Foy's assistance, including alternate rows of rock chestnut acorns, shagbark and black walnuts.

His next planting season began on March 18, 1828, and his pace increased. He put out seedling pots for a different variety of experiments, and planted in them post oaks, chestnut, shagbarks, plums, tamarinds, persimmons, grapes, oranges, apples, and pears. After a period of frosty weather during the first full week of April, JQA feared that the cold temperatures and frost had killed or seriously damaged most of his plantings. In consultation with Ouseley the gardener and his valet Antoine, however, they discovered that minimal damage had occurred. A month later, on May 5th, a hailstorm inflicted damage on the trees in his nursery.

JQA made many more subsequent plantings in the garden and nursery, including the following:

cork oaks	Spanish chestnuts	English walnuts	black walnuts
shagbarks	persimmons	catalpas	gleditsia
apricots	cherries	white mustard	raisin seeds
pignuts	Spitzenberg apples	gooseberries	almonds
grapes	strawberries	cherries	prunes

JQA also planted seeds from foreign plants that came to the White House in response to a circular letter sent to U. S. consuls around the world. There was no concern for invasive species in those days, based on having no education of the harm they cause to native species. JQA planted cork oak acorns and Spanish chestnuts from Bilbao and Malaga, Spain, respectively; Brazilian squash, beans, and flowers; Dutch elms from the Netherlands; and Tangier vines, figs, palmettos, wheat, barley, dates, and lemons. The figs failed, but everything else at least grew somewhat. He once again made exhaustive notes on the growth he noticed on a daily basis. In particular, he counted close to 200 trees growing from his plantings the previous fall.

On April 22, 1828, while walking around the Capitol Square, JQA met Foy, with whom he observed trees and plants within the square's enclosure. They included tallow tree, sour cherry tree, red bud, arbor vitae, and a few others.

On his trip back to Quincy, JQA stopped by a seedsman shop in New York City, and visited Prince's Garden on Long Island for the last time as President. By early August 1828, he was back in Quincy, building on his home garden and nursery. There, he planted peaches, plums, cherries, apples, pears, and grapes. He also noticed the growth of his previously planted oaks, walnuts, elms, peaches, and plums. In October, he once again went on rides and walks through the woods to collect more planting materials, but he did not record any more plantings in his diary, if he even accomplished any.

JQA traveled back to Washington in November, but this time as a lame duck President. He had lost the election to Andrew Jackson and was preparing to vacate the White House by March 4, 1829. In February and just before he left office in the first few days of March, he said goodbye to his domestics, and to John Ouseley and John Foy, who had helped him with his gardening, educated him on identifying trees and plants, and advised him on other aspects tangential to trees and gardens over the past four years. He also parted with his Belgian assistant Antoine Giusta, who had been with him since 1814, but was hired to stay on at the White House and work for Jackson as a valet. JQA remarked in his diary that, "This Separation from Domestics who have so long lived in the family is among the painful incidents of the present time." He had time only to observe the springtime blossoming around him. JQA stayed in Washington until June before returning to Quincy by the 18th.

For Future Generations

54

Illustrations

Double Blossom Peach, painted by Abigail S. Adams, April 3, 1828, courtesy of Adams National Historic Park

Tamarind and Persimmon by Abigail S. Adams, June 28, 1828,
courtesy of Adams National Historic Park

Pin Oak Leaf and Fruit by Abigail S. Adams, October 4, 1828, courtesy of Adams National Historic Park

White Oak Leaf by Louisa C. Adams, July 6, 1826, courtesy of Adams National Historic Park

The Old House, Peacefield, with Abigail Adams's wisteria climbing
toward the chimney, courtesy of the GNU Project

The United States Botanic Garden and the Capitol, engraving from
Picturesque America: Or the Land We Live In, Volume II, 1874

Aerial view of Oranienbaum in St. Petersburg, Russia, courtesy of German Wikipedia, 2006

Postcard of mountain laurels along the driveway of the Arnold Arboretum in Boston, Massachusetts, courtesy of the New York Public Library, 1908

Photograph of the Hortus Botanicus, or Physick Garden, in Amsterdam, Netherlands, by Jacob Olie, courtesy of the Jacob Olie Collection, 1902

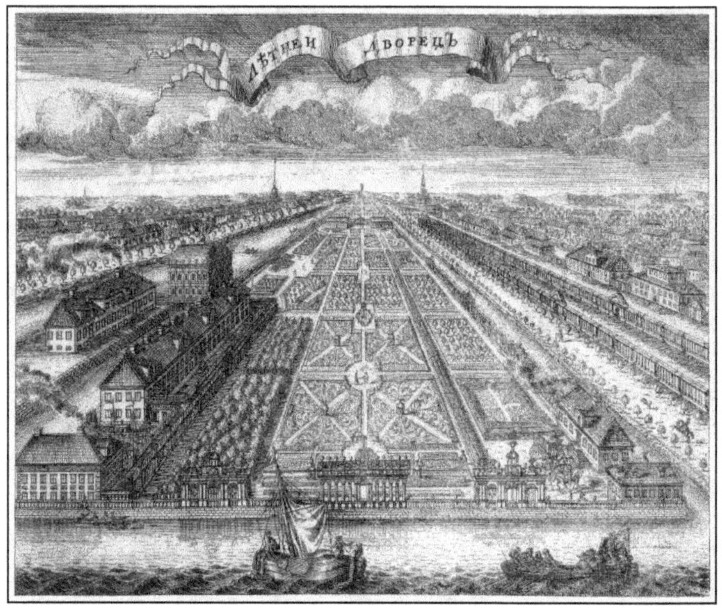

Summer House and Summer Garden in St. Petersburg, drawing by Alexey Zubov, 1716

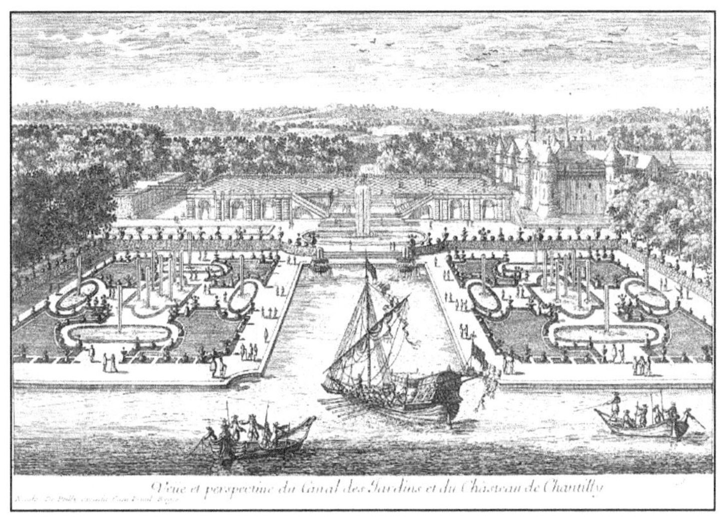

The Canal at the Domaine de Chantilly in Auteil, France, etching print by Pierre Aveline, 1685

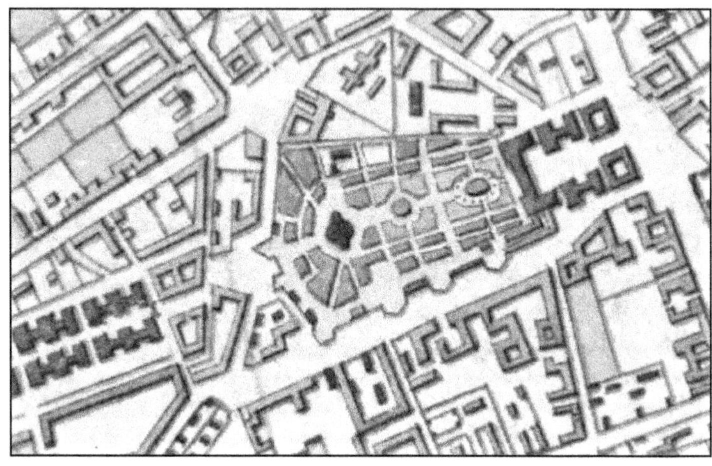

Schematic drawing of the Saxon Garden in Warsaw, Poland, by Josephinische Landesaufnahme, 1804

Portrait painting of John Quincy Adams holding a spyglass, by William Hudson, Jr., 1844, courtesy of the Smithsonian National Portrait Gallery

Oil painting of the John Adams Birthplace and John Quincy Adams Birthplace, by G. N. Frankenstein, 1849, courtesy of the National Park Service

Oil painting of The Old House, Peacefield, by G. N. Frankenstein, 1849, courtesy of the National Park Service

Full length portrait painting of John Quincy Adams, by Gilbert Stuart (head, 1825), and Thomas Sully (body, 1829-30), courtesy of the Harvard University Portrait Collection

Chapter 6: Presidential Activities

While JQA was President of the U.S., he was very active using the authority of his office in the collection and preservation of trees and plants. Throughout his presidency, he worked to reserve and preserve lands to use timber for naval ship construction, and for the enjoyment of future generations. He also worked with learned societies and his cabinet to collect diverse samples of botanic life from across the globe for their potential in education, science and commerce.

Prior to JQA's presidency, Congress and the U.S. Navy built a foundation of support to conserve trees for use in building naval vessels of all necessary types. It led to a 1799 act of Congress to authorize the President to purchase necessary lands on which timber grew for the future use of the Navy. That president was none other than JQA's father, John Adams, who purchased Grover's and Blackbeard's Islands   off the coast of Georgia, containing a total of nearly two thousand acres of live oak stands. The catalyst for additional conservation efforts did not come until the War of 1812, when President James Madison realized the need for a stronger Navy, and thus the need for more timber. On March

1, 1817, before leaving office, Madison signed The Timber Act, which was the first U.S. law designed at least in some manner to preserve trees on public land and protect against their depredation. James Monroe used the act to perform tree surveys of coastal Louisiana and Alabama in 1818 and 1819. On February 29, 1820, Monroe created the first naval live oak reservation from eight islands in Louisiana's Lake Chetimaches, now called Grand Lake. It turned out that no live oak timber was ever taken from these islands, and by 1832, the Navy ceased tracking the status of the live oaks there. After the acquisition of East and West Florida from Spain in 1821, Congress had to act again to prevent lumbermen from decimating the live oak timber in these regions. Monroe signed the Timber Preservation Act on February 23, 1822. Surveys were conducted, but the unauthorized cutting of timber continued in Florida for the rest of Monroe's presidency.

Not long after taking office, JQA began mentioning the preservation of trees, especially southern live oaks, in his daily diary notes, beginning in June 1826. He had surveys completed of South Carolina, Georgia, and Florida live oaks that year. By 1827, he was talking regularly with other politicians about preserving live oaks, especially Secretary of the Navy Samuel Southard, who was pivotal in partnering with JQA on the survey and preservation of southern trees. It was the Navy that JQA envisioned as the leading agency to preserve live oaks for shipbuilding, but he also was looking to future generations for enjoyment of these forests. On March 3, 1827, JQA signed into law "An Act for the Gradual Improvement of the Navy of the United States," which included the preservation of southern live oak forests. It was the foundation of all forest protection efforts from 1827 to 1861. The first reservation from the Act was 3,602.25 acres of red cedar trees in Monroe County, Alabama, adding to the live oaks already reserved by the Navy in Pensacola, Florida, which were enclosed in the land used to establish the Pensacola Navy Yard in 1825. Shortly thereafter, in May 1827, the Navy planted more live oak seedlings in Pensacola. JQA also had a discussion with William Pope Duval, the first Territorial Governor of Florida, on November 7, 1827, to synchronize on the measures necessary to preserve the live oaks in Florida. In March 1828, Southard convinced Congress to authorize purchase of more live oak land surrounding the Pensacola Navy Yard, and accomplished the purchases of 1,600 acres near Deer Point, Florida, the Santa Rosa Peninsula (1,600 acres), the Bayou Grande Tract (1,250 acres), and the St. Carolas de Barrancas Tract (800 acres), for a total of 3,650 acres. Prior to this, Southard had presented the purchase plan to JQA on January 28, 1828. As Southard awaited JQA's approval for making the lands official reservations, he purchased the two remaining tracts of land near the Perdido River and the Big and Rill Bayous. JQA was not able to approve the reservations before he left the presidency in 1829, but they were eventually approved, along with other reservations, by future presidents. The Deer Point tract eventually became the first operating federal tree farm in the U.S. on January 18, 1829, shortly before JQA left office.

The Deer Point Reserve contributed the lumber for the restoration of the *USS Constitution,* the revered Revolutionary

War heavy frigate that earned the nickname "Old Ironsides" for its impervious live oak hull. JQA actually received a naval inspired honor and gift in the early days of the debates that established the Smithsonian Institution. On June 1, 1837, at the Adams homestead, Peacefield, Nathaniel Thayer, a Unitarian minister and Massachusetts State Representative and Senator, and four others in a delegation from the Massachusetts House of Delegates, from towns within the twelfth congressional district, read an address to JQA "expressing their approbation of my [JQA's] conduct as their Representative in Congress," and presented a cane made from the timber of the *Constitution*[6], otherwise known as "Old Ironsides," the nickname it earned after defeating the *Guerriere*[7] in the early stages of the War of 1812. JQA accepted the cane, "the article not being of sufficient pecuniary value to decline upon a general principle." He bequeathed it in his will to his grandson, John Quincy Adams II, son of Charles Francis Adams.

By May 1827, JQA began discussions with the Columbian Institute for the Promotion of Arts and Sciences to distribute a circular letter to U.S. consulates around the world to send specimens of seeds and plants for growing in the Society's botanic garden, which eventually formed the foundations of the U.S. Botanical Garden. His participation in the Institute's establishment and activities were more

---

[6] The *Constitution* is the oldest commissioned U. S. Navy vessel still afloat, home ported in Charles Town Navy Yard, Boston, becoming a floating museum in 1976.

[7] The *Guerriere* was a French frigate launched on September 15, 1799, but was captured by the British on July 19, 1806. *Constitution* captured and burned it on August 19, 1812.

broad and influential, and came together with his presidency to greatly affect the nation's approach to appreciating and preserving trees and plants through the Institute.

The Columbian Institute established its constitution in 1816, as competition for the American Philosophical Society in Philadelphia. The second article of its constitution was the catalyst for their botanic garden, stating the goal, "to collect, cultivate and distribute the various vegetable productions of this and other countries, whether medicinal, esculent, or for the promotion of arts and manufactures." In 1818, the Institute received a twenty year charter from Congress, and in 1820, President James Monroe signed a congressional bill into law granting the Institute five acres in Washington, DC, to establish their botanic garden. The Institute elected JQA as their president in 1822, primarily for the vital role he played in the eventual success of the botanic garden. JQA left his role as Institute president when he became the U.S. President in 1825, and ended his membership shortly after leaving office in 1829. His primary reason for his departure which he wrote in his diary was that, "the principles of the present Administration were members, one member acting toward me as a willful and knavish slanderer, and two others returning my kindness and hospitality with personal disrespect and dishonorable political malice. I would not join any voluntary association with them."

The discussions on collecting plants for the botanic garden began in 1826, after the garden's property was improved with drainage, plant beds, walkways, and a 100 by 140 foot elliptical pond. Secretary of State Richard Rush developed the letter that would be sent both domestically and internationally to collect whatever plant life that could be obtained. The letter contained a description of JQA's endorsement and personal interest in the project's success. JQA had discussions with Rush concerning collection of plants and seeds from elsewhere, and the letter's development, from April to July 1827. He also put Rush and Southard together to strategize on the plan. The three men recruited several experts on the subject to discuss the best methods of collecting and transporting plants and seeds, and to review and comment on the draft letter. Experts included Dr. James Mease, doctor and horticulturist, who was an officer of the American Philosophical Society at the time; Dr. David Hosack, physician and botanist, who started the Elgin Botanic Garden[8] in New York City, the first public garden in the U.S., and tended the mortal wounds of Alexander Hamilton and his son Philip Hamilton after their duels; Dr. Jacob Bigelow, physician and botanist, a Harvard Professor at the time, and author of *American Medical Botany*; Stephen Elliot, South Carolina legislator, banker, educator, botanist, and author of *A Sketch of the Botany of South-Carolina and Georgia* (1816); Judge Henry M. Brackenridge, who would eventually become the superintendent of the Deer Point Live Oak Preserve; and Robert Carr, husband of Ann Bartram, daughter of John Bartram, Jr., second director of Bartram's Garden[9] in

---

[8] Hosack established the Elgin Botanic garden in 1801, but could no longer sustain it by 1810, selling the land to the State of New York. The land was given to Columbia College in 1814, which is now the site of Rockefeller Center.

[9] Bartram's Garden was established by Ann Bartram's grandfather John Bartram, Sr., in 1728, and is now the oldest surviving botanical garden in North America.

Philadelphia. Rush also pulled instructions for transporting plants over the sea from the writings of John Coakley Lettsom, English physician and entomologist. The letter, along with a second document describing transporting and handling of such plants, went to each member of Congress for their state's constituencies, the Secretaries of State, Treasury, Navy, and the Postmaster General. It was also published in the *National Intelligencer* newspaper. In addition, through discussions with Asbury Dickens, then the President of the Columbian Institute, and the drafting of a parallel letter, JQA kept the Institute in the wings during the fall of 1827 to potentially support the effort themselves as the first plants and seeds began to arrive.

In October 1827, and in some cases before the distribution of the circular letters late in 1827, JQA began seeing deliveries of those seeds and plants from the states and other countries, including the Netherlands, Spain, Brazil, Uruguay, and Tangier. Domestically, plants and seeds came from South Carolina and Alabama. Even though the Institute planted many of the deliveries in the botanic garden, JQA was sure to make a percentage of them part of his regular plantings at the White House.

A side effort in which JQA involved himself with the Columbian Institute was the development of their official seal. His recommended design, which he described in his diary entry of December 10, 1827, was of "a ship under Sail, encircled by a Constellation of twenty-four Stars beyond which an outer circle of clouds, and an external border: with the Words COLUMBIAN INSTITUTE on the upper part of the Circle, and XX APRIL MDCCCXVIII, the date of the Act incorporating the Institute, on the lower part—and with the Motto FULGENT SIDERA NAUTIS, from Horace Book 2, Ode 16 to Grosphus. The allusion of the device and of the Motto is to the Patronage of the Institute by Congress." He thought of his design as ingenious, though he admitted in a conceited way. The design that Asbury Dickens returned to him for his review the following February 21, 1828, had none of JQA's recommendations, instead having a rattlesnake coiled around a book with a different motto, both of which JQA found inappropriate but approved anyway.

On May 28, 1828, Sidney Breese, a U.S. Senator, Chief Justice of Illinois Supreme Court, Speaker of the Illinois House, and considered father of Illinois Central Railroad, paid JQA a visit and presented him with a petrified pear from Monroe County. The visit ended indifferently when Breese could not answer JQA's inquiry regarding whether or not petrification was common in that area.

As JQA left the presidency, events occurred that both ended and kept in motion his efforts to forward the importance of trees and gardens in the U.S. Although there is no concrete proof of intentional destruction, the party after Andrew Jackson's inauguration at the White House turned into an alcohol fueled soiree that ended with the trampling and ruining of JQA's garden and nursery. His valet, Antoine, unwittingly helped bring about the destruction by luring guests outdoors with the alcohol in an effort to avoid indoor destruction of the White House by the unruly crowd. In contrast, the Columbian Institute's botanic garden continued to thrive for another ten years until its own halt in progress due to the disestablishment of the Institute in 1837. It nevertheless laid the groundwork for the U.S. Botanic Garden, with the help of future efforts in which JQA lent an all-important helping hand as a U.S. Congressman.

For Future Generations

Chapter 7: Post-Presidency, 1829-1831

When JQA arrived in Quincy on June 18, 1829, after his departure from the presidency, he visited his nursery the following day, where he found nearly all of his seedlings dead due to harsh drought and heat. He managed to find three or four oaks still living out of hundreds, along with a few new peaches and plums that had broken the ground from pits planted the preceding autumn. Nevertheless, he began planting again a few days later on the 23rd. He concentrated primarily on planting many chestnuts and apples in June through September. JQA was still receiving seeds and nuts from U.S. Consuls as a result   of his circular from 1827. He and son John planted chestnuts from Constantinople (now Istanbul, Turkey) and lima beans from South America sent to him by Edward Wyer. Wyer was the former U.S. Consul to Riga, capital of Latvia, which was then a territory of the Russian Empire, and to Hamburg, the second largest city in Germany, which was then a sovereign city-state of the German Confederation.

On July 17th, JQA walked to Boston publisher and neighbor Thomas Greenleaf's house, touring his gardens and observing many exotic trees. The next day, he took a trip to Medford, Massachusetts, north of Boston, to visit the gardens of Edward Brooks, the son of Peter Chardon Brooks, the wealthiest man in the state at the time, and soon to be father-in-law to JQA's son Charles, who married Peter's daughter and Edward's sister Abigail on September 29th. Three weeks previous, on June 29th, JQA had walked up the hill from the Old House with the two Brooks gentlemen where he showed them the plot of land where he planned to build a new house, which would be the spot where his son Charles would actually build his house in 1836. The elder Brooks recommended that JQA begin by planting trees. He visited the elder Brooks, who had become ill, and toured his gardens on September 4th, where he found a great number of flowers, bushes, forest and fruit trees, both foreign and domestic, along with a greenhouse and a bridge that Brooks had built over the Middlesex Canal[10] which bordered his property. Later that month, on September 23rd, while visiting his brother Thomas Boylston Adams, JQA found Thomas's brother-in-law, Charles Harrod, there, who gave him willow, water oak, and shagbark acorns, along with honey locust and jasmine seeds from Illinois. Harrod was the president of Atchafalaya Bank in Louisiana, and aid to General Andrew Jackson during the Battle of New Orleans in 1815.

During the entire month of October, JQA got back into the business of surveying lots of land he owned, most inherited from his father. There were inaccuracies in the

---

[10] The Middlesex Canal was built between 1793 and 1803, operating until 1851 when railroads took away most of its practical usage. It connected the Merrimack River to the Port of Boston.

1826 surveying just after his father's death, which caused a number of disputes with neighboring landowners. It all began on August 28th when, while visiting Elisha Turner, the husband of JQA's first cousin Mary, Elisha's brother Peter Turner alerted him that Deacon Spear, the administrator of the estate to JQA's uncle and Mary's father Peter Boylston Adams, wanted to confer with him on the true title of certain wood lots. JQA met with Spears the next day, when they agreed the appropriate time to survey the lots was in October or November. The lots had interesting names, some matter-of-fact and some imaginative, including the following:

Rock Common Wood	Lawyers Common	Quincy Meadow
School-House Lot	Penn's Hill Orchard	Atherton & Verchild Lot
Fresh Meadow	Goose Pasture	Penn-ferry Lot
Cherry-tree Stump Lot	Pinehill Woodlots	Town-river Marsh Lot
Savil Lot	Large and Small Owen Lots	Beale Lot
Borlund Lot	Babel Pasture	Four Basswood Trees Lot

The process ended with all lots settled in their ownership, and an auction of the Lawyers Common lot on November 6th, as well as several sly attempts from gentlemen trying to make deals with JQA on other lots of land and the chopping down of trees for wood fuel. JQA was concerned that these gentlemen may be too sly and take advantage of him, but he was able to withstand their flattery and make no deals. He said of a potential sale and cutting of an old oak that "the sight of it was worth more to me than six dollars."

JQA stayed in Quincy until late in December, arriving back in his Washington home on the 30th. It was a row house, which greatly limited his Washington, DC, gardening ambitions. But he stayed there until late May 1830, staying close to the political action in the city. He arrived back in Quincy on June 2nd. His planting maintained a high level of activity, including the following seeds, nuts, berries, and acorns:

walnuts	peaches	cherries
currants	whortleberries	pears
limes	thimbleberries	apricots
apples	blackberries	plums
basswoods	willows	water oaks
huckleberries	horse chestnuts	black & white oaks

He also transplanted apple trees into his nursery, began experiments by steeping seeds in New England rum, and began planting in book boxes he had brought home from Washington. The summer house cellar was full of young seedling trees ready for transplanting. His nursery began to come back into flourishing life. He counted 106 trees growing again. His more mature fruit trees began bearing fruit, including cherries, apples, and pears, some of which he gathered and took to the Boston Market to sell.

On June 17, 1830, JQA wrote a lengthy entry in his diary discussing his plantings, fretting about the many ways they can perish, and the difficulty he had in paying enough attention to their needs. He also wrote of visiting his next door neighbor, George W. Beale, a good farmer who gave much advice on the dangers of insects to plants and trees. He was inspired upon his return from Beale's gardens to lay out his thoughts for the future:

> "It would be worthy of the Agricultural and Horticultural Societies to institute formal researches and inquiries into the natural history of fruit trees, and of the insects that prey upon them. For myself, I shall probably continue, as long as my life and my health will admit to sow and plant every summer seeds, stones, and acorns, the trees from which will continue to perish by frost and by sun, by insect and by disease, all for want of continued attention and systematic pursuit. I am yet convinced that much useful service to the country might thus be performed by the raising of forest trees; but it would require a permanency of property not adapted to our political Institutions and Laws; with as each generation looks only to itself."

On August 6th, JQA and Louisa visited Nathaniel Frothingham, pastor of the First Church of Boston, and his wife Ann, a daughter of Peter Chardon Brooks, in Medford, on their way back from seeing the Bunker Hill Monument, which was not yet completed and would not be until 1843. He toured the grounds, observing old shellbarks over a century old in 1830, and requested a bucket of acorns from Frothingham's large white oak tree. A few days later, on August 12th, JQA continued to receive seeds for planting when neighbor Daniel Greenleaf gave him lime seeds and cherry stones (he also managed to visit Daniel Greenleaf's grounds a month later on September 16th and inspected his oak and walnut trees). After planting some of the seeds and stones two days later, JQA was inspired to quote Roman comic poet Statius Caecilius in his poem *Synephebi* ("Fellow Adolescents"), comparing the planting of trees to the planting of laws and institutions:

> "'He plants trees for the benefit of another century; for what purpose, if the next century were not something to him. The diligent husbandman, then, shall plant trees upon which his own eyes shall never see a berry; and shall not a great man plant laws, institutions, a commonwealth.' I have had my share in planting laws and institutions according to the measure of my ability and opportunities. I would willingly have had more. My leisure is now imposed upon me by the will of higher powers, to which I cheerfully submit, and I plant trees for the benefit of the next age, and of which my own eyes will never behold a berry. To raise forest-trees requires the concurrence of two generations; and even of my lately-planted nuts, seeds, and stones, I may never taste the fruit."

Another neighbor, Rufus Davis, brought horse plums to JQA on August 17th, which he planned to plant, not eat.

While walking through the nursery with son Charles on August 22, 1830, JQA made his first mention of planting a fruit tree orchard on one of his farm lots, to both begin a fruit selling business, and create a monument of trees for future generations to sustain and enjoy. Within the next month, in fact within a week of first mentioning it, he decided upon his Mount Wollaston farm as the location for his orchard, and chose the precise location for it on September 11th. He chose a pasture on the southern facing side of Mount Wollaston. On September 23rd, he went out to the farm and, with his tenant Alpheus Spear, had it measured out in a rectangle 540 feet long and 379 ½ feet wide, about two acres.

On the last day of August, before the orchard began to take shape, JQA strolled over the hill to a place he called "the old trash garden spot" to observe whatever may be growing there from times past. He found a bounty of trees, including forty hickories and five or six shellbarks with many nuts. There were many cedars as well. He also found a large black oak, two smaller ones, a juniper tree, and three or four each of elms and pear trees. There were so many trees that JQA concluded that the spot was turning into woods. Wild cherry trees that he had known to be growing there were bearing fruit, but were not yet ripe.

One misadventure JQA had during the month of September was an attempt to plant a patch of flint corn, which he called Indian corn, within the nursery. After its successful growth and bearing of corn, a striped squirrel had begun to eat its fill of the bounty. JQA's frustration with the furry thief was thought to have ended when his hired gardener, Solomon Farrar, shot the squirrel in the corn patch. A short time later, however, the theft continued and expanded to the devouring of cabbages. Farrar tracked down three more squirrels, but JQA became relegated to the fact of his corn remaining a treat for all local creatures, and began calling it "the squirrel corn patch." While summarizing his activities for the month, JQA looked forward with cautious hope that his experiments and efforts would carry his ambitions to future generations:

> "My series of experiments is neither scientific nor perhaps judicious, but the thought that the result of them may be useful hereafter to others sustains me in pursuing them. The reflection which most weighs with me is that if it had commenced in my youth, and steadily persevered into this time, I should now be reaping a harvest of abundant fruits, and enjoying perhaps, the shade of a lofty forest – That which now might have been mine, may with the blessing of Heaven be the comfort of my grandchildren the next century; and if there be to the all-seeing eye and the all-controlling will, presumption in the wish, there yet may be other future human beings, whose enjoyments will be increased by my plantations."

He repeated these hopes again in mid-October, and during the month, he took walks along different paths in his wooded lots, as well as around the town and other neighborhoods, to find acorns, nuts, and fruit, or simply to observe the variety of trees. He also converted a plot of land in the Old House's yard which he called "The Stony Barren" into another plot to grow young trees and plants. Once it was suitable for planting, he began calling it "The Seminary."

He finished the conversion by October 13th. A few days later he visited retired General Henry Dearborn, senior officer of the U. S. Army during the War of 1812 and Thomas Jefferson's Secretary of War, in Roxbury. The two men discussed trees, and JQA received stone pine seeds from the Mediterranean region. Later that month, JQA commissioned a letter seal to be made that had an acorn surrounded by two oak leaves, and the phrase "Alteri Seculo" on a banner below the acorn, which translates from the Latin to "For Future Generations." He used this seal on his letters for the rest of his life. Now, the Quincy House at Harvard University uses a very similar symbol as their house logo.

By October 21st, JQA observed the ploughing of the orchard grounds, and on October 23rd, he began tree planting. It was primarily an apple orchard, with one border of adult oak trees, and three borders of alternating chestnuts, oaks, and shagbarks, which he planted from the acorn and nut. JQA and his hired farmers finished the planting of the orchard by November 27th, which included seedling apple trees purchased from a traveling farmer, from a Medford orchard, and seeds JQA planted himself. Upon the orchard's completion, JQA once again waxed almost poetically about the potential future of his works:

> "Mount Wollaston has belonged to my ancestors and to me about 190 years. That is from the settlement of Braintree to this day…It is now pregnant with at least ten thousand seeds of fruit and forest, mostly planted by my hand, and in a century from this day, may bear timber for the floating castle of my country, and fruit for the

subsistence, health, and comfort of my descendants. To all which the blessing and sanction is indispensable of the giver of all good, and which with humble diffidence and hope, I invoke."

His orchard ambitions did not slow down his plantings in his nursery. In fact, in addition to the plantings he accomplished up until September 14th, he planted every day after that until November 22nd, with the strongest push beginning on November 3rd. He even performed a last bit of moving seedling trees into the summer house cellar and protecting the roots with nursery earth on November 29th and December 4th. It was the heaviest planting and trench digging workload he ever accomplished during any time in his horticultural career. He found that, overall, his trees were flourishing in a greater abundance than they had ever done before. One of the features he set upon for the nursery was a row of shellbark trees to grow where he planted them without transplantation, along the western wall of the nursery.

On October 25th, a man named John Jones rode by with what was left of a wagonload of chestnuts from New Hampshire, which he was selling. He asked to see JQA in the nursery, and was thrilled by the sight of him, stating that seeing him was more rewarding than selling his chestnuts. He told JQA that he had worked for his father John Adams on the Peacefield farm, and lived there more than twenty years previously.

In the same period of time, political activities came back into his life when he had his first discussions with local politicians about taking over the vacant seat of the local U.S. Congressman on September 17th. By October 13th, he decided to accept the nomination, but claimed that he did not pursue it intentionally. On November 6th, the newspapers showed that he had won the election. After a few more fall plantings in November, he headed back to Washington on December 8th, arriving on December 17th. On Christmas, he purchased a gift for himself in the form of *Evelyn's Sylva*, a multi-volume set   of books known as one of the most influential texts on forestry ever published. It was written by English writer, gardener, and diarist John Evelyn, first published in 1662 with multiple editions published over the next nearly 200 years.

JQA returned to Quincy on April 30, 1831. His interest remained in his botanical pursuits, and did not waiver during the time in Washington. He did not make nearly as many plantings as the previous few years, but with so much growth in his garden, nursery, seminary, and orchard, his observations took most of his time. His reputation began to spread as well, and he began receiving seeds, nuts, and small plants from people both local and distant on an almost daily basis. His friends, neighbors, and relatives became invested in JQA's enjoyment and hopeful success of plantings. He planted thimbleberries, nectarines, peaches, currants, and oaks. He was able to transplant pears, horse chestnuts, and cherries from his summer house cellar, where he conducted most of his experiments. One of those new experiments was creating hybrid plants by splicing a twig of one plant onto the stem   of another. Many orchard trees were growing, his apples and pears were growing, and many experiments were coming up. However, for the time being, he concluded that his apple seed plantings were a failure, since only around twenty had broken the ground since the previous autumn. He realized that he had planted many of them too deeply to survive the trip to the surface. He still made many visits to his orchard. JQA's son Charles had also taken an active involvement in the nursery, garden, and orchard, bringing plants from his local travels, and writing in his own diary about it. Nevertheless, JQA still fretted about his success or failure, and even compared the raising of trees with the raising of humans:

> "I have often thought that a man should guard himself against all propensities – I found this however as impossible as to make my oak trees grow up straight – They will take bents by nature – They will receive biases from external pressure – It is almost as difficult to educate a tree as a child."

JQA also did more reading, including *The Transactions of the English Horticultural Society*, Scottish gardener and botanist John Claudius Loudon's *Encyclopedia of Gardening*, and Scottish arborist Thomas Cruickshank's *The Practical Planter,* which he had obtained from General Dearborn to borrow during a follow-up visit to his property. He read and wrote much about *The Practical Planter* in his diary each day. On July 9, 1831, JQA was made an honorary member of the Boston Horticultural Society, and received a diploma to mark the occasion. One other thing that he did was prepare for his congressional career. After putting Farrar in charge of his various plots of plantings, and wondering in what shape they would be upon his return, he traveled back to Washington on October 28th, unofficially beginning his career as a U.S. Representative from Massachusetts on November 13th, and being sworn into office on December 5th.

For Future Generations

94

Chapter 8: Congressional Gardening, 1832-1848

Although JQA no longer had his White House garden and nursery, he still worked in the small garden he had at his Washington, DC, house during the first half of 1832, but only mentioned it once in his diary on June 19th, reporting that he found all of the strawberries gone when he visited the garden. Most of his time was consumed with congressional thoughts and activities. He did, however, have time to bathe in the Potomac River with John on June 17th, but found that all of the trees that provided shelter were gone from the rocky point where he would normally enter the river.

JQA left Washington on July 17th, arriving back in Quincy on July 26th during the congressional recess, as he would do every year. He checked his nursery on August 3rd, and found most seedlings killed again primarily by the previous harsh winter, but new shoots coming up from his plantings of the previous fall. His orchard did not fare much better, but the border trees were thriving, if they could survive the many weeds he noticed growing up around them. He felt like he had been in a six-year apprenticeship of raising trees, and had learned nothing. He became "despairing and aimless" in his gardening, and made visits more rarely this summer and fall. He did find, however, a growth of young oaks in his Sawyer's Common Lot, and auctioned off the adult trees for firewood, and to give the younger trees more room to grow. He also pruned existing trees and planted more limes, cherries, pignuts, currants, white beech, horsebean, chestnuts, white oaks, and strawberries.

On August 24th, he passed through Daniel Greenleaf's property and examined his trees, noticing a white beech bearing nuts, and red oaks coming up from acorns that Greenleaf had planted the previous summer. Back at his own gardens, he had hired a gentleman named Simson Taylor the previous autumn for their maintenance and care, who, on August 27th, was replaced by Henry Wentworth. He left Quincy on November 8th, and arrived in Washington on November 15th. During his time in Washington, family illnesses and congressional occupations prevented him from working in his house garden, walking, and observing vegetation virtually the entire time.

JQA traveled to Quincy on April 11, 1833, arriving on April 20th. Many of his trees were dead or sickly. Almost all of his orchard seedlings had perished, but the garden and nursery were doing better. He noticed that red oaks and elms were coming up, and one nectarine and six peaches bore fruit. He only had time to plant more strawberries and cherries, and transplant cedar seedlings. After one of his visits, he became thoughtful of his experiences once again, and recorded those thoughts in his diary on May 8th:

> "My experience convinces me that the only proper mode of raising trees, whether for fruit or for the forest, is from the seed; but that it is an art, requiring skill, and a continued course of minute observation – a long and persevering pursuit of the object – patience in waiting for results – fortitude to bear disappointments with good temper, and judgment and reflection to draw profitable facts from observed phenomena – after six years of persevering experiment, I am yet to learn how to sow or plant the seed, so that my considerable portion of it shall come up – and how to protect it when up from the frost – from the heat of the sun; from insect and from mice."

JQA began visiting his garden, nursery and orchard twice a day, spending up to four or five hours examining the growth and shape of his plantings. He mentioned in his diary on June 7th that his interest in trees began in his early youth, but the course of his life did not allow him to pursue it for a considerable number of years. On August 5th, JQA developed a boil on his hand which threatened to end his gardening for the year. From August 29th to September 8th, he took a convalescent trip to the White Mountains of New Hampshire. Along the way, JQA observed, "Oats, rye, flax, and buckwheat, a very few orchards, and occasional moderate sized beeches, oaks, and maples, with white and pitch pine, cedar, and hemlock. The next day, upon returning from the trip, JQA found that he could still do no gardening, but a visit from Deacon Spear entertained him with the story of how he Became John Quincy Adams:

> "Deacon Spear told me that my father had related to him the anecdote of the manner how my name came to be John Quincy – It was the name of my maternal great grandfather. I was born on Saturday the 11th of July 1767. My mother's mother, Elizabeth Smith, wife of William Smith, Minister of the First Perish of Weymouth, was with my mother at the time of my birth. Her father John Quincy was on his death bed, and she requested that his name might be given to me, which it accordingly was on Sunday the 12th of July. My great grandfather died the next morning, in the 79th year of his age."

By September 13th, he was doing some gardening again. He found that he had a few successes in his plantings by way of ripe dwarf apples, nectarines, and peaches. When November came, he worked as hard as he could to transplant seedling trees into the garden and nursery that he felt were ready for such movement, as well as to take potted flower indoors for the winter. By November 6th, he left Quincy, arriving in Washington on November 10th. Once again, he spent no time on his house garden, perhaps leaving it to a hired gardener. He did, however, notice that on March 2, 1834, the weather was so warm that some trees were already beginning to bear leaves.

JQA left Washington for Quincy on July 5, 1834, arriving on July 13th. He noticed that buttonwoods, willows, honey locusts, and oaks were growing in his nursery, but not much else. There were some trees from one to six years of age, and more seedlings were growing. He worked an average of two hours a day in the garden and nursery, primarily through observations, mentioning almost no planting related activities. He did comment on his continuing experience, saying, "The art of the nursery and seedsman to make tall and strong stems to their seedling trees, I still lack." The orchard was picking up, but only on one border. JQA paid a visit with son Charles to Price Greenleaf's plantation nursery on August 18th, observing many old trees, and flowers mixed in with young trees. In October, the steady growth of the chestnut trees in his orchard gave him a feeling of "eminent success." He had counted three hundred trees on three sides of the orchard, other than the western side, which had not succeeded as well. JQA had planned to plant more orchard trees, but on the evening following his orchard observations, he received a message that his son John was gravely ill in Washington. He left Quincy on October 19th, arriving in Washington on the 22nd. John died on the 23rd from the effects of alcoholism. After the funeral, he used his congressional work as a shelter from his grief.

JQA left for Quincy again in mid-May 1835. On May 21st, while stopping in Philadelphia, he toured Bartram's Garden along the Schuylkill River, which was open for only seven years at that time, but is now the oldest public garden in North America. He saw "multitudes of beautiful flowers" and exotic trees. As he entered New England, particularly in Providence, Rhode Island, he noticed the blossoms everywhere, including the apple orchards, lilacs, and horse chestnuts,   of which he enjoyed their appearance and fragrance.   Once he arrived in Quincy, he found many nursery trees killed and dug up accidentally by a stranger who someone put in place to tend to JQA's plantings, but it was still like a little forest. The orchard looked better as well, especially the border trees. On June 25th, he ate cherry tarts and strawberries from the garden, writing that they were very good.   He planted apples, pears, plums, cherries, apricots, and peaches. He also transplanted oaks, walnuts, elms, and chestnuts into the orchard. One tree that he acknowledged was a walnut that he had planted thirty years before, and was one of the largest trees on his property.   In mid-July, JQA began calling the portion of his garden and nursery where he installed shingles to shelter seedling trees from the sun his "seminary." He had begun this type of protection in the summer of 1834, but applied it in earnest in the sun-drenched heat of 1835.   He also enjoyed watching the hummingbirds feed on the nectar   of the althea flowers blooming outside of his bedroom windows.

On August 24th, the growing success of his tree plantings in the garden, nursery, seminary, and orchard inspired him to philosophize over the feelings he gained from the growth of trees:

> "In the innumerable disappointments which befall me since this plantation fancy came over me, these occasional incidents of success not only more than balance them with pleasure, but afford a continually repeated enjoyment, delusive indeed like all the pleasures of the imagination, but which occupy and pleasingly

agitate the mind – When I lose a plant, especially one which I have cherished, and enjoyed in hope, the painful sensation is ridiculously acute, but is momentary and soon forgotten; but the plant that comes up; that grows from day to day the first season, and from year to year afterwards is a continual feast, and as it grows and gives growing hope of proving hereafter useful by producing fruit, it affords enjoyment not unworthy of a rational being – I cannot bring myself to take much interest in flowers, because they pass off and perish, leaving nothing behind – but the trees now seemingly as effervescent as the petal of a rose, and which yet on hundred years hence will bear delicious fruit, or afford a shelter and a shade to after ages of men – these yield me delight."

The same day, JQA observed a walnut tree he had planted thirty years previously, with its descendants growing all around, and commented on its beauty and usefulness. A few days later, he observed an elm that had grown from an old stump as little more than a twig, and seven years later was a considerable tree. He also recruited his granddaughters Mary Louisa and Georgiana Frances to plant with him. On September 14th to 21st, he took a family trip to Nantucket, making sure to record the types of trees he saw on the trip. In the first few days of November, he added to his orchard by having his nephew John Kirke transplant from his garden and nursery fifteen English oaks, twenty seedling walnuts, twenty elms, and four horse chestnuts. By

November 11th, he was on his way back to Washington, arriving on the 14th. It does not appear that he did any planting or tending to his house garden during this latest stay in Washington.

In 1836, JQA left Washington on July 6th, arriving in Quincy on July 13th. Along the way, he stopped outside of Philadelphia to visit Nicholas Biddle, President of the Second Bank of the United States, at his estate, Andalusia[11], on the Delaware River. He toured the grounds and observed the trees and gardens the next morning before returning to the city. He found his nursery and garden "in tolerable order." JQA visited his garden and nursery before dark the same day he arrived in Quincy, and was disappointed in the lack of last year's plantings coming up, but there were 600 trees on the orchard border, and the nursery was full of trees, with no room left for more plantings. It was a great fruit bearing year. He also marked ten years of growing seedling trees, and the fact that he absorbed hours of his time each day merely gazing in fascination at his seedling trees. He made no plantings this summer, but he created seedling circles for his two granddaughters to begin a planting hobby.

JQA's son Charles took seedling oaks to transplant at his house up the hill from JQA. On September 3, 1836, the anniversary of the Treaty of Paris and Charles' marriage, JQA gave to him, "the seal which by my father's direction, I had engraved at London in 1815 with his device of the deer, the

---

[11] Andalusia was built by original land owner John Craig in 1794, and designed by Benjamin Latrobe. Nicholas Biddle married Craig's daughter Jane, and worked with Thomas U. Walter (designer of the Capitol dome) to greatly expand Andalusia in 1834-1846.

pine tree and the fish, surrounded by the thirteen stars by which in 1783 he commemorated the rights of the fisheries and of the boundary, secured by the treaty of peace with Great Britain....It has on the other side of the stone the Adams arms...I had already on the 27th of October 1833 committed in trust to Charles for the remainder of my life the Lion crested seal-at-arms of the Boylston family, with which my father sealed the treaties of 30 November 1782 and 1783."

After making his final plantings of the season, JQA began the return trip to Washington on November 8th, arriving there on the 10th. Once again, he appeared to have not done any gardening during this stay.

He left Washington on May 10th, 1837, arriving in Quincy on May 15th. He found great destruction of nursery trees. The orchard needed lots of work, but it was growing well. He gave up on most of his fruit tree planting, and spent the entire time in Quincy working on the nursery and orchard. On August 4th, a highlight of the summer came when JQA's cousin Josiah Adams gave him a cane composed of twenty-five different kinds of wood strung upon an oak staff and glued at the joints, retaining all of the natural colors of each kind of wood used. He left Quincy on August 29th, arriving in Washington on September 2nd. A horticultural highlight of his time in Washington came on July 7, 1838, when he met Dr. Henry Perrine, U.S. Consul to Campeche, Mexico, and proponent of introducing tropical plants into the U.S., at the chamber of the U.S. Committee on Agriculture, and examined the tropical plants that Perrine had brought from Mexico.

In 1838, JQA left Washington on July 17th, arriving in Quincy on the 19th, ending his longest stay in Washington. He found good growth in the nursery, still calling it a forest, including "several maple trees from Philadelphia sown 1 June 1835 flourishing beyond all comparison, one of the trees at least 12 feet high – shagbark hickory trees 5 years old and promising – a considerable number of peach trees, some of them well stocked with fruit – here and there an oak from 2 years old to 10 – a few equivocal apple trees...". He discovered his orchard was planted over with potatoes by the tenant farmer. His amusement for planting had nearly vanished at the start of his stay, but by August 24th, his desire began to return. It was probably his discovery of many trees still growing in the orchard, and a large yield of apples and peaches that brought back his enthusiasm. He also managed to plant more seeds, nuts, acorns, and stones, though he did not specify which types.

On October 4th, JQA visited the local engraver who had engraved his acorn letter seal to get the words "alteri seculo" sunk a bit deeper into the metal, so that they would appear more clearly in sealing wax. At the end of October, JQA wrote his usual monthly summary of his activities in his diary. This was the first monthly summary entry that did not include trees and gardens in many years. There seemed to be a shift of his interest during September and October to astronomy, probably brought on by discussions he had in Congress on using the financial bequest of deceased British scientist James Smithson, which would lead to the creation of the Smithsonian Institution, for a national observatory. He began reading astronomical texts daily, and making morning observations   of stars and planets. Astronomy had actually been a parallel preoccupation for JQA since the 1820's, but the following decade would concentrate his powers of rhetoric and persuasion for astronomy to its pinnacle. It would result in JQA's indispensable influence on the creation of the Harvard College Observatory, the Cincinnati Observatory, the U.S. Naval Observatory, and the Smithsonian Institution. At the end of his planting seasons, he stayed in Boston for two weeks with son Charles before traveling to Washington, arriving on November 28th.

1839 was a bad year for JQA's trees and his personal life. He arrived back in Quincy on May 2nd, and found many of his nursery trees lost. His gardener, John Kirke, had uprooted approximately 200 of his nursery trees and carelessly transplanted them in the orchard. Still he was able to obtain 159 young apple tree seedlings and had them planted in the orchard to restart his project. In May, however, he expanded the seedling circles for all six of his grandchildren. In July and August, he had no time for further gardening after becoming obsessed with organizing his many papers and books, which had accumulated since he was president. He still managed to observe garden peaches, cherries, plums, lilacs, and tulips blossoming, and his granddaughters' peach, pear, and apple seedlings coming up. On September 26th, he visited the exhibition of the Massachusetts Horticultural Society, "where there was a fine display of flowers, fruit, and culinary esculents." However, things turned sour again later that day when he discovered that cows let loose in the orchard by a tenant farmer uprooted the potatoes and corn that had been planted there.

Then, on November 20th, his nine-year-old granddaughter Georgiana died of a brief and mysterious illness. Her decline prevented JQA from being able to concentrate at all on his garden and nursery, passing the final 1839 plantings over to John Kirke early in the month. After Georgianna's funeral, there was nothing left to do but go back to Washington, which he did on November 27th.

JQA did not return to Quincy until August 1, 1840. Although he was still working in the garden and nursery, his plantings began to become reduced. On August 4th, after visiting the seedling circles of his grandchildren, he spilled out his emotions concerning Georgianna's death and its inextricable connection to his love of trees:

> "The anguish of her long protracted suffering and that frightful creeping upon her of death, from hour to hour for weeks and months in succession disqualified me for all energetic action and extinguished almost all the interest I had so long taken in the cultivation of trees. There upon the small plats in the seminary which I had specially given to her, and in which she took delight – There were various seedlings upon them, now entirely overgrown with weeds, except one peach of the second year of stunted growth. On the other a black currant yet stands and bears the first berries, with an unthrifty apple seedling at its side – a self-planted violet covered it with blossoms through the whole of the last summer, and there is a remnant of them there now – Oh, if I could describe the sensations

which I feel on looking upon those two plats, it would be conceived how all the pleasure has vanished with which I was wont to look at the plats which I had given to each of my other grandchildren, as tokens to them of kind remembrance of me, when I shall sleep with their and my fathers. I have thought it would be to them a pleasing though perhaps melancholy recollection – I did not think of the withered violet – the flower out off in its bloom – Was not this trial fixed upon me as a warning?"

JQA still managed to plant peaches, plums, shagbarks, and white oaks, and made detailed lists of his observations. Charles also began supporting his father with plantings and had built his own interests. From September 1st to 19th, JQA and his son worked on taking a trip to Halifax, Nova Scotia, but had to cut it short when the ship they planned to use was badly damaged and threatened to strand them for a long period of time if they did not return on the ship that brought them from Boston on the first leg of the trip. Upon their return, Georgiana's death still greatly affected him when he wrote concerning his visit to the seedling circles, "I cannot approach the plat but with sweet and bitter tears." At the end of the month, he decided to leave the maintenance and management of the Mount Wollaston, Penn's Hill, Mansion House farms, and the Saltmarsh and Woodland lots to his son Charles. Then, in October and November, lecturing for his position as the Professor of Rhetoric and Oratory at Harvard University, along with congressional work from his home, kept him from his gardening. He left Quincy on November 15th, arriving in Washington on the 23rd.

JQA returned to Massachusetts in late April 1841, but stayed with his son Charles until May 16th in Boston. Once back in Quincy, he noticed that there were dozens of apple trees up from his plantings of the previous fall, and the peaches, plums, and cherries were blossoming. His granddaughters' seedling circles now had three years of growth for their trees. He was also able to plant a few oaks and shellbarks in the garden. He did not stay in Quincy for long, however. By May 29th, he was back in Washington to stand before the Supreme Court to argue the historic case of the enslaved Africans who overpowered the crew of the ship *Amistad* to gain their freedom. JQA won the case, and was back in Quincy by September 23rd. This time, he found that drought and insects had ravaged his plantings. Nevertheless, he planted black oaks, peaches, and shagbarks.

On September 27th, JQA discussed in his diary a visit from Mr. and Mrs. Charles Downing. Downing was an influential botanist and horticulturist from Newburgh, New York. He had written *A Treatise on the Theory and Practice of Landscape Gardening, Adapted to North America* (1841), which he dedicated to JQA. He occupied himself for the rest of the season with regular visits to his plantings, reading, and making almost daily astronomical observations at his son Charles' house during walks. He then stayed in Boston with Charles from the 10th to the 29th of November, before being back in Washington on December 1st. During this stay in Washington, JQA traveled to Fairfax, Virginia, and visited

Sharon[12], the residence of U.S. Navy Commodore Thomas Ap Catesby Jones and his wife. He called it "a paradise in the wild," surrounded by trees filled with the songs of birds.

He did not return to Quincy until September 9, 1842. By this time, almost all of his seedling fruit trees had perished, but his nursery trees were still flourishing, including oaks, shagbarks, walnuts, maples, and apples. He managed to plant white oaks and horse chestnuts, but no other plantings this fall. He also granted trees to the local episcopal church for transplant. JQA stayed with Charles in Boston from November 21st to 29th, and then took a short trip to Providence, Rhode Island, to visit with friends before traveling to Washington, arriving there on December 2nd.

JQA stayed in Washington until May 2, 1843, arriving in Boston on the 5th, and staying until the 16th, when he wrote in his diary upon arriving, "I have returned once at least every year for the last 15 years, to this calm retreat from public labours and boisterous passions with extesy of delight..." He commemorated his years of planting by counting 100 trees still growing on his property, and noticing that one of his maples was now 25 feet tall. He still visited his garden and nursery every day, planted apple and cherry seeds, and transplanted some apple seedlings to save them from the drought of that year. On May 26th, he toured the tulip gardens in Roxbury, Massachusetts, closer to Boston than Quincy, but still south of the city. He took a side interest in the songs of birds on June 24th, noticing the

---

[12] Thomas Ap Catesby Jones inherited Sharon from his mother in 1810. The mansion was demolished in 1963 to make way for the Broyhill Estates planned neighborhood.

bobolink, robin, sparrow, quail, blackbird, bluebird, and swallow. Then, from July 6th to August 5th, he and the family took a vacation to Niagara Falls, riding the Western Railroad. On the way through New England and New York, he felt that it looked like a Garden of Eden, "charged with a variety of fragrances." He observed fields of Indian corn, rye, potatoes, oats, and orchards laden with ripening fruit. They next day before reaching Niagara Falls, he saw a contrasting region of dark forests. In Lebanon, New York, they took lodgings at the foot of mountains where JQA saw that they were covered with oak, chestnut, beech, birch, black walnut, and sugar-maple trees, with willows, sycamores, sumac, and locusts interspersed among them. Once at the falls, which they saw from Goat Island, JQA was destined to meet Ormsby McKnight Mitchel, an Ohio astronomer, who asked him to lay the cornerstone of the Cincinnati Observatory. He took the offer, and by September 27th, he had returned to Quincy and was on his way to Cincinnati. He made a speech in favor of astronomy and laid the cornerstone in a ceremony on November 9th, returning to Washington for the new congressional season on November 23rd. Before that, on August 3rd, during the return trip from Niagara Falls, the traveling party stopped in Albany, New York, and visited Rensselaerswyck, the mansion house of Stephen Van Rensselaer IV, whose late father was a former Lieutenant Governor of New York. While there, JQA toured the elegant gardens and greenhouse.

JQA returned to Quincy on July 13, 1844, where he saw more devastation from frost and drought over the previous winter. During the trip home, in Jersey City, New

Jersey, JQA stepped accidentally off of a raised platform at the train station 4 feet off the ground and fell, pulling Louisa with him, since she was holding his arm. They fortunately were not injured seriously other than bruising and the severe jostling they received. It took nearly two weeks, however, for JQA to recover from a deep thigh bruise well enough to return to manual labor in the garden and nursery. He still worked to save what was left of his plantings, noticing that there were still many apple seedlings in his summer house cellar. He also planted plums, shagbarks, pears, and apples, and moved pear and apple seedlings from the summer house cellar to the nursery to begin filling it again. In addition, he read Sir Francis Bacon's *Sylva Sylvarum*, his most read natural history, published after his death in 1626.

On October 25th, after his daily walk in the garden and nursery, he walked up the hill to Charles' house to watch the sun set, but walked on over the hill to settle on a prospect giving him a wide-ranging view of the town, the Bay of Boston, the state house, and Bunker Hill Monument. His thoughts progressed from the past to the future, whence he related his mixed feelings about the unknown and what he had accomplished:

> "The recollection of the past is pleasing and melancholy; the prospect of the future—oh, how gloomy it is 1 Not a soul now lives who was then in the bloom of life. Not a soul now living will be here in 1924. My own term— how soon it will close! And to whom will all this belong in eighty years from this day? Will prayer to God preserve the branches and shoots from

my father's stock? What a phantasmagoria is human life!"

By November 18th, JQA left Quincy and arrived in Washington on November 23rd.

On May 3, 1845, JQA returned to Boston and stayed at Charles' house until May 23rd, when he returned to Quincy for what would be his last year of working in the gardens. He observed a lovely spring, with his maple trees flourishing. He made another detailed list of the items growing, but especially singled out his favorite shagbark and a 40-year-old hickory tree that was bearing nuts. He also planted cherries and plums, and transplanted mulberries, white maples, and willows. On June 3rd, JQA received from Commissioner of Patents Henry Ellsworth ten small parcels of seeds including corn, rye, beans, beets, Connecticut squash, Bocharia melon, and Essex spring wheat. He planted them in accordance with the instructions included from the Patent Office. Two weeks later, he noticed a catbird, robin, and bluebird take turns eating their fill of fruit in his trees, concluding that they needed the fruit more than he did. On September 22nd, after once again developing a boil on his hand, his work in the garden ended for the season, and he was relegated to touring and observing only.

In the fall, JQA sent chestnut, apple, and shagbark trees to the horticulturist Andrew Jackson Downing in appreciation of dedicating his most recent book, *The Fruits and Fruit Trees of America,* to JQA. On October 18th, JQA seemed to have made his last entry on gardening in his diary after the boil that had given him trouble a few years earlier had returned on his hand. He ended up staying with Charles in Boston from October 22nd to 28th, went back to Quincy for a few days, then stayed in Boston again from November 5th to 27th, arriving in Washington on November 29th.

JQA left Washington again on August 13, 1846, arriving in Quincy on August 16th. There was no more gardening, but much more stargazing. He had become passionate about astronomy while in Congress, and was very influential in the development of observatories at Harvard University, Cincinnati, and the Naval Observatory in Washington. He left Quincy on November 18th to stay in Boston for a time, but had a stroke on November 20th. He convalesced at Charles' house for the rest of the year, but was able to go outside by New Year's Day 1847. On January 22nd, he began taking short walks around the neighborhood, and by February 8th, he was able to travel, arriving in Washington on February 12th.

JQA left Washington on June 1, 1847, arriving in Quincy on June 5th. Gaps began to appear in his daily diary, including a significant chunk of that summer, from June 12th to August 9th. He left Quincy for the last time on November 1st, arriving in Washington on November 5th. Then, on February 21, 1848, JQA suffered a fatal stroke and cerebral hemorrhage while deliberating on the floor of the House of Representatives. He was taken to the Speaker of the House's room, where he died two days later on February 23rd. His last words were, "This is the last of Earth. I am content." One of those present was the young congressman from Illinois, Abraham Lincoln. After lying in state in Washington, being temporarily interred at the Congressional Cemetery for one week, and a train trip back to Quincy that showed how much the country adored him, he was buried there on March 4th. In 1852, he was reinterred in the United First Parish Church, his final resting place with wife, Louisa, and parents John and Abigail Adams.

JQA left a rich legacy of trees and gardens for the enjoyment, use, and entertainment of the United States. The Adams' home, Peacefield, still contains the gardens and remnants of his tree nursery, where at least 42 fruit trees and many nut and acorn trees still flourish. Many groves of live oak forests still grow across the southern states. One of his elm trees survived on the White House lawn until 1991, which was then replaced by a seedling from the same tree by First Lady Barbara Bush. He even facilitated the foundational plantings of what became the U.S. Botanical Garden. And generations of Adams family gardeners and arborists kept up his work to at least some degree, which is what he really wanted all along.

Chapter 9: Partners in Planting

JQA had many partners throughout his years of growing trees and plants. Some were neighbors, some were hired, some were partners of circumstance, and some were family. The following is a list of those most prominent partners with a brief description of how they worked with JQA.

- Antoine Michel Giusta: JQA hired Antoine as a valet in 1814 while in Belgium. Antoine stayed on with JQA, came back to America with the family, and stayed with JQA until hired by Andrew Jackson at the White House in 1829. While with JQA, he planted, transplanted, spade up weeds, procured planters like glass tumblers and flower pots, and was successful in his personal plantings. He even married Mrs. Adams' maid. Years later, the maid visited the Adamses in Quincy, and let them know that Antoine had traveled to Michigan to do land speculating, where she eventually joined him.

- John Foy: Foy was the Arborist for the U.S. Capitol, and is regarded as the first U.S. public gardener. He came to Washington, DC, from Kentucky in 1819, recruited by Henry Clay, who at the time was the Speaker of the House of Representatives. Soon after JQA became President, he began discussing trees with Foy and convinced him to support his efforts in creating a tree nursery at the White House. Foy was pivotal in constructing the nursery. He did much of the tree plantings, and also agreed to maintain the Columbian Institute's Botanic Garden, which eventually evolved into the U.S. Botanical Garden.

- John Ouseley: Ouseley was the White House Gardener, appointed on August 1, 1825, and someone who JQA called "a living, walking dictionary of plants." Ouseley was an Irishman who emigrated from Waterford, Ireland, to the U.S. in May 1818, first settling in South Amboy, New Jersey. He moved to Washington, DC, in 1825, and achieved naturalization as a U.S. citizen on May 25th of that year. JQA himself hired Ouseley as White House Gardener. He took many walks and had many discussions with JQA, imparting his knowledge of plants. He also maintained many of JQA's experiments and seedlings while maintaining the White House garden.

- Joseph Elgar: Elgar was a surveyor by trade who first became the Surveyor of Montgomery County, Maryland. He later became a clerk under Samuel Lane, the Commissioner of Public Buildings for DC. In 1817, Lane forced the incumbent Surveyor of Washington, Benjamin Latrobe, out of office and replaced him with Elgar. By 1822, upon Lane's death,

Elgar became the Commissioner, later to be renamed Superintendent   of Public Buildings in Washington. His partnership with JQA was mainly for the purposes of settling disputes among gardening, landscaping, and construction, not the least of which was the relationship between the Columbian Institute Botanic Garden and the layout   of other public buildings in Washington. Elgar fenced in the nursery at the White House. He was also knowledgeable about the laws and rules for laying out gardens, and supported JQA in this way.   He remained as the Commissioner of Public Buildings until 1834.

- John Adams II: JQA's middle son went on many walks and horseback rides with his father on various jaunts in Quincy and Washington, DC, collecting twigs, acorns, nuts, and seeds. These trips also afforded time to observe forest and ornamental trees.   He also supported the surveying of JQA's woodlots.

- George Washington Adams: JQA's eldest son, like John, rode with his father, collecting twigs and acorns, and observing trees. He went with his father on a few of his garden visitations and tours. George supported JQA with his plantings in the garden and nursery. He also procured some of the books on trees and gardening that JQA would read.

- Solomon Augustus Farrar: Farrar was a hired workman of JQA's father, John Adams, whom JQA put to work tending to the gardens and orchard at

Peacefield from time to time. He also supported the surveying of the various Adams lots of land. Farrar even leased some   of JQA's land to do his own farming.

- John Kirke: Kirke was a distant relative whom JQA hired to support his garden, nursery, and orchard. Although he was supportive of JQA, he also committed some of the most costly mistakes that damaged and destroyed JQA's seedling trees at times.

- Louisa Adams and Abigail S. Adams: JQA's wife and niece provided their own special support to his efforts. Besides the usual support that a wife and niece provide to their loved ones, both Louisa and Abigail created lovely paintings of flowers, leaves, and plants that grew and were collected around the property, and were beyond reach for JQA's close study.

Beyond these partners, there was one other who affected, and was affected by, JQA like no other when it came to raising and caring for trees and gardens. JQA received support from all of his sons in various ways while pursuing his botanical interests. George Washington Adams and John Adams II accompanied him on his visits to gardens both domestic and international, and helped him with his plantings in the garden, nursery, and orchard. But it was JQA's youngest son, Charles Francis Adams, who inherited the most interest in trees from his father. He strongly supported his father's work in his later years, maintained

JQA's orchard and gardens when he was in Washington, transplanted young trees to his own property, and developed his own orchard in later years.

Charles was born in Boston on August 18, 1807. At two years of age, he traveled with his parents to St. Petersburg when his father was appointed the U.S. Minister to Russia. Charles lived in Europe until the age of ten as his father moved from St. Petersburg to Ghent, Belgium, to negotiate the peace treaty for the War of 1812, and to England as the U.S. Envoy to the United Kingdom. As early as 1814, Charles professed his botanical desires to his father in a letter from St. Petersburg to Ghent, writing, "I came to Mama's Country house last Saturday. There is a very small Garden, in which I play; Mama is going to give me some seeds to sew, and I hope to become quite a Gardener. I have already got a Spade, a Rake, and a Wheel-barrow." JQA replied to the letter by writing, "I am very glad that you have a Garden to amuse yourself in, and that you have a Spade, a Rake and a wheelbarrow, to teach you gardening and give you wholesome exercise—And by the time you receive this Letter, I hope your seeds will have come up, and shewn you the process of vegetation."

The family returned to the U.S. in 1817 when President James Monroe appointed JQA as Secretary of State. Like his grandfather and father, Charles earned a bachelor's degree from Harvard University. He then studied law under Daniel Webster in Washington, DC, between 1825 and 1827. He afterwards returned to Boston and opened his own law practice. Charles married Abigail Brooks in 1829. He was a Massachusetts State Delegate from 1840 to 1842, and State

Senator from 1843 to 1845. He unsuccessfully ran for vice president with Martin Van Buren in 1848, and for Massachusetts governor in 1876, but he was a U.S. Congressman from 1859 to 1861, being elected twice. He then became the U.S. Envoy to the United Kingdom from 1861 to 1868, once again like his grandfather and father before him. In 1870, he built the Stone Library on the grounds of Peacefield, the first presidential library in U.S. history. He also became one of the leading historic editors of his time, completing the bulk of the diary and biography of his grandfather, John Adams, which his father had begun, and publishing the voluminous diaries of his father. Later in life, he was bestowed a fellowship in the American Academy of Arts and Sciences.

It was not long after his graduation from Harvard that Charles was well involved in the botanical interests of his father, and developing his own pursuits, primarily with trees. On August 31, 1827, he wrote in his diary, which he had begun in 1820, that he was learning how to bud fruit trees. JQA was anxious for Charles to learn this process, and sent Price Greenleaf, the nephew of his neighbor Daniel Greenleaf, to teach Charles how to bud.

The following spring, in April 1828, Charles began in earnest to study the raising of trees, most likely due to the projects with which his father required assistance. He was reading about agriculture and the planting of trees, but concluded that active participation was more valuable than reading. On April 15th, he traveled to General Dearborn's orchards, who had agreed to provide JQA with a large number of trees to begin his own nursery at Peacefield. After obtaining the trees, Charles set to work planting one row of forty English oaks, and, in three additional rows, fifty-three elms. The trees had been growing for approximately three years. He also planted eight elms, eight buttonwoods, and a few shellbark acorns and pecan nuts as experiments. He concluded that it had been a good day's work.

By June, Charles found that his plantings were a complete success, all of the trees having taken root, and still maintained their health the following spring. He also read industriously about trees from volumes borrowed from his father, including André Michaux's *The North American Sylva*, and Philip Miller's *Abridgement of the Gardener's Dictionary*. Both volumes are now held in the Stone Library. The next month, after observing damage that had been done to JQA's peach trees, Charles wrote the first critical passage in his diary concerning his father's skills as an arborist, stating, "And my father, although a fine theorist, has not the least practical and useful knowledge in the world." This probably came from his observations of his father's techniques that left more to be desired in the success of his plantations, such as the planting of different seeds and nuts on top of each other in the same place, and the digging up of seeds, stones, and nuts out   of impatience to discover their progress.

The following summer, on August 22, 1830, Charles made an interesting claim concerning the creation of his father's Mount Wollaston orchard. He felt that JQA was close to going ahead with the orchard, but wrote that it was his proposal, not his father's original idea, to create the orchard. In contrast, JQA's language in his diary leads the reader to believe the idea of an orchard had been percolating in his head until he decided to go through with it. On the same day, JQA wrote that he proposed picking a spot for the orchard to Charles. In fact, a few days later, on August 27th, they went together to pick a spot, but did not quite complete their mission. On September 11th, JQA chose a pasture on the south side of Mount Wollaston, and showed it to Charles on October 3rd. Whichever way it initially developed, Charles was back to his readings by September to prepare for the moment when JQA gave the green light to the orchard. On the same day as JQA's choice of the pasture, he received a letter from Charles, who was at his Boston home, describing the advice he had received from his father-in-law, Peter Chardon Brooks, to take up trees for the orchard in the fall and plant them in the spring.

Later in September, Charles went on a short trip in order to observe trees for their own sake. He walked to Woburn with his father-in-law to a locally famous elm tree on the farm of Abel Richardson. The two men performed a measurement of the tree's circumference two feet from the ground, finding it twenty feet, three inches. It was said to be 136 years old at the time of their measurement. The following day, they walked to Boston Common in order to visit another elm that rivaled the Woburn elm in age and girth. Their measurement this time was nineteen feet, three inches, not quite as large as the Woburn elm. Brooks, however, had recorded in his farm journal in 1825 a measurement   of twenty-one feet, eight inches, which said something about the consistency of measurement procedures between the two expeditions.

A day after the elm measurement expedition, on September 22nd, Charles took Brooks with him to Warren's Nursery in Medford to make a definitive contribution to the creation of the Mount Wollaston orchard. He purchased eighty budded Baldwin apple tree seedlings at twenty-five cents apiece. He most likely made at least one additional purchase that he mentioned on November 24th. The orchard was established by the close of the 1830 fall planting season. The following spring and for a good portion of the remaining months in 1831, Charles made many visits to the orchard with his father to inspect its status. JQA was hopeful of growing his son's interest in late 1830, but began to realize his actual interest and involvement in the spring of 1831.

Beginning in 1832, since JQA had begun his congressional career, Charles increased his caretaking of both the house and the grounds at Peacefield. He took greater action in transplanting and pruning trees planted by JQA, himself, or the various men working for them. He had a portion of the garden reserved for his work with raising strawberries and raspberries. He also had deliberate strategies in mind when planting trees, such as shading the rear of the house, or creating a welcoming appearance with trees along the driveway and front of the house. On April 24, 1832, he was inspired to write in his diary, "I think this year and the last have done a good deal in the way of improving the old mansion. It looks more like a Gentleman's place." By the fall, although the trees had suffered from drought in the spring and summer, they were looking better, and the beauty of Mount Wollaston stirred the first notions in Charles of having his own house there someday.

In the spring of 1833, the orchard and nursery looked even worse, and both JQA and Charles were concerned for the survival of the trees. To supplement the continued beautification of the Peacefield grounds, Charles purchased and planted ten maples, ten firs, ten spruces, and ten white cedars shipped from Maine. On October 15, 1834, JQA sent Charles to a Medford engraver with a plate of a white oak leaf from one of his books as a model for the creation of his "alteri seculo" letter stamp. Over the course of 1833 and 1834, Charles continued his regular visits and work in the garden, nursery, and orchard, which held out in a condition of steady state, but did not exactly flourish. He also continued his dreams of having a house on Mount Wollaston. That dream became a reality in 1836, when construction was completed on what Charles called "The New House," juxtaposed with Peacefield, which JQA called "The Old House." It was built on Mount Wollaston, as Charles had wanted. It did not take him long to begin arboreal designs on the plot of land. For close to a week in October, beginning on the 22nd, he took firs and pines from his father's nursery that had been growing for years, planting them on his new property, especially on the southwest side of the house stretching north as a windbreak against the northwest winds. On the west side of the house leading further up the hill, he planted a total of fourteen elms, with one ash, one buttonwood, and three oaks. JQA also took it upon himself to plant a walnut tree at each corner   of Charles's property.

The previous year, in June 1835, JQA discussed his desire to build a stone library on the Peacefield lot as a fitting place to store the family writings and correspondence.

Charles had trepidations at this proposal, due to his desire to begin building his own house and place the library there, but agreed with the plan to build it at Peacefield. His house would be built the following year, but Charles did not fulfill the plan for the library until 1870.

Charles and his family lived in The New House, which is now known as the Adams-Angier-Powell House due to subsequent owners, until 1849, after JQA's death and his inheritance of The Old House in 1848. He also purchased a Boston rowhouse at 57 Mount Vernon Street in 1842, where the family alternately lived thereafter for the rest of their lives.

In the fall of 1836, on Charles's birthday, JQA presented him with John Adams's letter stamp which incorporated a deer, fish, and pine tree, signifying the elder Adams's reverence for nature. Charles continued his tree ambitions the following month, October, when he took up a number of oaks and elms that had overstayed their time in JQA's nursery, and planted them at his house.

The following spring of 1837, Charles planted more trees on his property, some of which he obtained from his father-in-law's farm. That summer, he engrossed himself in a book by Sir Henry Steuart, *The Planter's Guide*. He was particularly interested in learning about the transplanting of large trees. He was able to put this knowledge to use in 1839 when JQA's garden overseer, John Kirke, tore up a nine-year-old white oak, which Charles took to his house and planted, in an attempt to save it. The book also provided knowledge on soil types, weather exposure, and treatments for tree ailments.

By 1840, JQA left much of the lot maintenance for his properties to Charles, who eventually leased JQA's Mount Wollaston and Penn's Hill lots to tenants in 1841. During the last few years of his father's life, Charles continued to care for Peacefield, and participate in his father's horticultural activities, an example of which was their visit to the Walker Garden in Roxbury, Massachusetts in 1843. JQA succeeded in passing along his passion for trees and gardens to the next generation, as Charles maintained his interest until his passing in 1886 in Boston. It was not the end of Peacefield's stewardship by the Adams family. Charles's son Henry Adams inherited it from him, and made his own lasting marks on the landscape of the estate. Peacefield did not leave the possession of the Adamses until 1927, when it was sold to the Adams Memorial Society[13]. In 1947, it was acquired by the National Park Service, becoming a National Historic Site.

---

[13] Brooks Adams, son of Charles Francis Adams, established the Adams memorial Society in 1926 and converted The Old House to a museum.

Chapter 10: Prose on Planting

When JQA's passion for planting was at a peak level, he could become nearly poetic in the emotional prose he wrote in his daily diary throughout his life. Examples can be found in nearly every stage of his botanic pursuits.

After a walk with his son George on October 16, 1806, he wrote philosophically of his connection to the land and imparted that connection to his children to carry it into the future; "This afternoon I took George with me over part of the farm with the view to familiarize him at this season of his life with the scenes upon which my own earliest recollection dwells – I feel an attachment to these places more powerful than to any other spot on Earth, precisely because they are associated with the first impressions of which the traces remain upon my mind – These attachments are connected with some of the sentiments and opinions which I most cherish, and which I should wish my children to possess."

During his time in Russia, he took many walks in the Summer Garden at Peterhof in St. Petersburg, and he said as much on October 7, 1811 by writing that the gardens had given him "frequent and agreeable walks the summer through." They actually gave him years' worth of these walks.

After arriving in Ghent, Belgium, in 1814 for the War of 1812 peace negotiations, JQA observed the fields of wheat, rye, barley, and flax; "They appear now in their fullest beauty, some of them almost ready for the harvest, the others less advanced, but all waving above the ground and in their fairest verdure."

On July 26, 1826, JQA compared his multi-disciplinary schedule with the flight of the hummingbird; "Visitors consume unreasonable portions of Time, and besides my father's papers, Plants, Insects, the Stars, and endless genealogies distract attention, and waste hour after hour— I spent also this morning about two hours, where another Parterre [a garden arrangement] employed me like the humming bird in the Althea trees before my window — They fly from flower to flower, always on the wing, inserting their long bills into the cup, and never remaining more than from five to ten seconds at any one flower." The day before, however, he was still enthralled by his natural surroundings; "I give some attention also to the plants and insects which are swarming at this Season and the Natural History of which is full   of wonders."

That fall, on October 6, 1826, after settling his deceased father's estate, JQA wrote of his emotional upwelling upon what he thought would be the last time he ever set foot on the family homestead, concerning which he was fortunately very mistaken; "I left it with an anxious and consoling hope   of returning to it as to my own, probably within three short years, and of finding within the means and opportunity   of employing the remnant of time allotted to me on earth, in exercises of filial reverence and affection, of usefulness to my children, of benevolence to the neighbourhood of my own and my father's nativity, and of ultimate improvement to the condition of my Country— To as much of this as may obtain the approbation of higher power, I implore the directing and effecting hand of Providence— For so much of it as may be destined to disappointment, I pray to be prepared and resigned."

Through late March and early April of 1827, upon his return to Washington, DC, JQA colorfully described the new spring growth of the trees in the local area, including the following turns of prose; "the Lombardy Poplars are now shedding their blossoms which are disposed like a brush round a stalk 2 1/2 inches in length flexible as a worm," "The Peach trees in our Garden appeared first this morning in their blushing honours," "Of the young trees set out round the public buildings, the Tulip is next to the willow putting forth its leaves— The Sycamore shews nothing yet but swollen buds," "The process of vegetation was manifested upon many trees…the first of which are now full dressed in the verdure   of Spring," and concluding, "I have marked the order in which the trees falling under my observation put out their leaves. The variety in their manner of vegetating is so remarkable that I am humiliated by the heedlessness with which I have suffered this process to pass at least fifty times before my eyes without bestowing a thought upon it."

Late that spring, on June 12, 1827, JQA was inspired by observing the progress of an apple pippin working off its shell; "The process of vegetation, like all the works of Nature is astonishing when observed in its continual progress."

In the fall of the same year, on November 12th, JQA finished planting the final border of his White House tree nursery with oaks, shagbarks, pignuts, black walnut, chestnut, persimmon, tulip-tree and lime. He wondered about the nursery's posterity; "I indulge the imagination and the hope that this border will outlast many Presidents of the United States—but who can look into futurity for the natural life of a row of Oaks? and who can tell how soon they may be uprooted?"

His diary was not the only place that he deposited colorful language about trees and flowers. In one of his first letters from Europe to his brother Thomas Boylston Adams on April 11, 1778, transferring his thoughts to paper had not quite become second nature to him, and he tended to be somewhat repetitive in his terminology, as he wrote, "I Went about the City which we found very fine for there are many very fine public Walks in the City fine Rows of trees in the Gardens which made it appear very fine." A few years later, in a letter to his mother in 1785, while traveling from Auteuil to Dreux, on the road to Paris, JQA showed improvement in his prose and wrote, "The roads from Paris here, are vastly agreeable; the ground has not yet, the true tincture of green; but almost all the trees are in blossom, and exhale a fragrance, which would perhaps have had a poetical influence upon me, if my Spirits had not been too low: the dust, was not so inconvenient, as I had feared."

JQA could also be playful in his language regarding trees and gardens, and who better to be the receiver of his playful language than his wife Louisa, as these passages demonstrate from a letter to her on May 31, 1804 while traveling from Quincy to Washington; "I wish we could have here a little of that superfluity of rain which fell just before you wrote me; as it would bring forward my *garden stuff* as we call it... Several of my peach-stones which I planted last September have come up; and I pay so much attention to the poor Plants from hour to hour, that the only danger is of my killing them all with kindness." He could also blend his love for her with his observations of nature in the seasons, when on August 26th of the same year, he wrote; "I hail the approach of Autumn as it draws near the time when I hope again to meet my best beloved, the separation from whom has become heavily irksome to me."

In his July 4, 1831 Independence Day address in Boston, JQA used botanic allusions to describe the growth of the nation; "The root struck from the seed of the Mayflower, and the plant ascending from it—salutary, fruitful, perennial. It shall rise to heaven and overspread the earth."

That October 29th, while traveling from Dedham, Massachusetts, to Providence, Rhode Island, on his way back to Washington to begin his first term as a U.S. Congressman, observed the surroundings of his native land and once again became inspired in his diary; "I pointed out to her [Susan Roberdeau, widow of General Isaac Roberdeau] the last view of the blue hills as they are seen from the borders of Dedham and Walpole, and fell into a reverie, enquiring of myself what it was that gave to those hills such power of touching sensibility as I always experience at their first and final appearance coming to or going from home – I traced the sensation to the spot of my nativity at the foot of Penn's Hill."

On June 22, 1839, after reading and accomplishing nothing else that day, JQA used the allusion to the hummingbird from years past to describe himself; "I can compare myself to nothing but the humming-bird which visits my althaea-trees in August, when they are in full bloom, buzzing upon the wing from cup to cup without alighting anywhere, and sipping liquid honey with a long needle beak from the bottom of each cup."

By July 1, 1843, JQA had taken a more relaxed and appreciative view of his orchard, nurseries, and gardens, showing this in his diary entry for the day; "In ranging round my grounds every morning, not a day passes but I meet with some new phenomenon of vegetation."

JQA sometimes used gardening as allusions to other efforts in "Letters to My Children," an 1809 collection of passages meant to teach his children how to properly handle various situations in life, JQA compared the particular attention paid to one division of topics in life and the "extraordinary toil and care" spent to the "cultivation which a thrifty and industrious farmer would bestow upon his garden." He also used these allusions to profess his love to Louisa. In a letter of August 26, 1804, from Quincy to Washington, he wrote, "The leaves are already changing their hue, and dropping from the trees—I hail the approach of Autumn as it draws near the time when I hope again to meet my best beloved, the separation from whom has become heavily irksome to me."

Whether it was writing for his own record, writing to his loved ones to keep them up to date on his activities, or writing as a means of communication with his colleagues and constituents, JQA incorporated his passions for each subject he communicated. Trees and gardens were no exception, and possible received more of his writing energy than most topics in his prose over the years of his life and career.

For Future Generations

Chapter 11: Legacy

JQA's nearly life-long dedication to trees and gardens survived long after his time on Earth, some artifacts of which still exist today. They appear at the family homestead, at the home of his son Charles, at local, state, and national parks, and in museums. Possibly the most important artifacts are the ones that still live.

Though many of the trees and plants he raised and nurtured at The Old House, Peacefield, have long disappeared, there are survivors of the past two centuries that remain as witnesses and beneficiaries of JQA's care. In 1830, JQA and Louisa planted a Yellowwood tree in the southwest garden after the death of their son George. They purposefully planted it in line with the upstairs window where Louisa had a writing desk, and could see it as she wrote. As told through generations of the Adams family, JQA and Louisa brought the tree from their Washington, DC, home. It still survives at The Old House, though it is in decline. One of JQA's favorite black walnut trees, which he planted in 1808 and called a shagbark walnut, survives in a healthy condition at the northwest corner of what was his tree nursery. At the western boundary of the property, there are hackberries, black oaks, elms, shagbark hickories, and linden trees. JQA planted the oldest trees, while Charles planted younger ones, and the Adams National Historic Park team planted the youngest. A mature elm that JQA planted still exists near the duck pond, while at least two others stand among trees surrounding the entry and garden area at the front of the property. Shortly after completing construction of a carriage house in 1873, Charles planted maples, beech, elms, and horse chestnuts on its western side which still exist today. Other nursery trees survived until at least 1936. A photo from that year showed seven trees including American elms, hackberries, and a white ash, which were all gone by a 1969 photo.

Trees grown from seedlings by JQA, but transplanted and cared for by Charles, still grow at both his house, The New House[14], and The Old House. In the Mount Wollaston orchard area, there are still sixteen apples, six pears, two mulberries, one hackberry, three walnuts, one catalpa, and one elm. Some of these trees may be JQA seedlings transplanted by Charles Francis, but there are no dependable records as proof. Also at The Old House are elms, yellowwoods, beech, maples, ash, and horse chestnuts that Charles planted on the east lawn which have since been thinned by park management over the years. Still surrounding Charles's house, there are beech, hickory, and oak trees that he transplanted from his father's seedlings.

---

[14] The property is now known as the Adams-Angier-Powell House, recognizing subsequent owners.

There are even survivors still existing from his parents' era, which JQA and subsequent generations maintained as part of their dedication to botanical pursuits. Abigail's wisteria still grows nearly the entire height of the chimney side of the house. Lilacs that Abigail planted grow on each side of the path from the gate to the front door. There are also two sweet bay magnolias from the Abigail and John era growing in the garden along the fence facing the road. In 1788, Abigail and John brought roses from England to plant in the garden; a red rose bush that represented the House of Lancaster, and a white rose that represented the House of York, primary combatants during the British Wars of the Roses from 1455 to 1487 for control of the throne. The Adamses retained the Lancaster and York names for their roses over the years. The York rose still lives today, but the Lancaster rose declined and died over the years, eventually replaced by the park team.

JQA's botanical legacies remain visible through his years of work with learned societies during his time as President of the U.S. and as a congressman. The Columbian Institute for the Promotion of Arts and Sciences maintained its botanical garden until 1837, when it disbanded, due to lack of financial support and the expiration of its twenty-year congressional charter. The Institute nevertheless continued to exist as a static entity until 1841, when it merged with the Historical Society of Washington, which had been established five years previously. The botanical garden transitioned to the oversight of the federal government, and stayed that way until 1850, when Congress began a search for space to house the botanical collection brought back by the U.S. Exploration Expedition (U.S. Ex. Ex.). This expedition, led by Navy Lieutenant Charles Wilkes and sometimes called the Wilkes Expedition, sailed the globe between 1836 and 1842, exploring, charting, and collecting objects and plants from around the world, as well as making geographic discoveries. It collected over 10,000 plant specimens and seeds, and more than 250 living plants. One of the scientific corps of the expedition was botanist William Brackenridge, the commissioner of the Deer Point Naval Live Oak Preserve.

Upon the expedition's return, Brackenridge received approval from Congress to build a fifty-foot long greenhouse on the grounds of the U.S. Patent Office to house and care for the living plant collection. The collection, along with other artifacts from the expedition, were cared for under the auspices of the National Institute for the Promotion of Science, which had been established in 1840 to house artifacts of national importance, and became the foundation of the Smithsonian Institution. At the same time, the National Institute was receiving other plant specimens, which quickly overcrowded the original greenhouse. Within a year, two additions needed to be added to house the growing collection. Five years later, in 1849, a new site needed to be found for the expanding collection, based on Brackenridge's success at multiplying some species of plants, which added to the volume. The site selected just happened to be the original location of the Columbian Institute's botanical garden, at the east end of the Washington Mall, beginning at the base of the Capitol. The U.S. Botanical Garden was established by 1850, with specimens collected from the JQA initiated circular letters, the Columbian Institute, of which JQA was President from 1822 to 1825, and the Wilkes Expedition, which was supported by JQA as a U.S. Congressman. At least one specimen in the U.S. Botanic Garden, the large Vessel Fern, is believed to be a survivor of the U.S. Ex. Ex. The Smithsonian Institution also received immense support and advocacy from JQA during the congressional debates to develop the course for applying the bequest from James Smithson, the English scientist who left a path in his will to provide his fortune of more than half a million dollars to the U.S. for "an establishment for the increase and diffusion of knowledge among men."

Like the lasting legacy of the botanic gardens, JQA also began a perpetuating legacy of live oak preservation in the southern U.S. The live oak stands that JQA reserved and endorsed for purchase became the Naval Live Oak Plantation at Deer Point in 1829. Their preservation endured, and in 1971, the National Park Service included it in the establishment of the Gulf Islands National Seashore, which preserves the natural resources around the Gulf of Mexico barrier islands of Florida and Mississippi. The Monroe County, Alabama, red cedar acreage was not as fortunate, as Twelfth U.S. President Millard Fillmore removed these acres from reservation in 1853, and Nineteenth U.S. President Rutherford B. Hayes sold them publically in 1880. Nevertheless, nearly every President from Andrew Jackson to James Buchanan applied the bill that JQA signed into law to preserve additional acres of not only live oaks, but yellow pines as well. Not all of those acres endured. In fact, large tracts have become the victims of clear cutting, industrialization, and urban sprawl. The live oak reservation system came to a halt through the start of the Civil War, most reservations being seized by the confederacy, and the sharp decline in the need for wooden hulled ships, which were being replaced by ironclad hulls. In 1880, the reservations were transferred from the Navy to the Department of the Interior, which managed to preserve a percentage of the reservations. The following tables depict in a general sense the reservations applied, the year they were reserved, the size reserved, and the present condition of the reservations, linking each to an authoritative organization carrying on their oversight and conservation.

<u>John Quincy Adams</u>

Original Reservation	Tree Type	Current Reservation	Authority
Monroe County, AL 1828 3602 acres^	Red Cedar	none	Hayes administration sold publically in 1880
Santa Rosa Peninsula, FL*@ 1828 1600 acres	Live Oak	Gulf Islands National Seashore, 1971 135,458 acres	National Park Service
Bayou Grande Tract, FL* 1828 1250 acres	Live Oak	Gulf Islands National Seashore, 1971 135,458 acres	National Park Service
St. Carolas de Barrancas Tract, FL* 1828 800 acres	Live Oak	Gulf Islands National Seashore, 1971 135,458 acres	National Park Service
Deer Point, FL* 1828 (purchased only) 1338 acres	Live Oak	Gulf Islands National Seashore, 1971 135,458 acres	National Park Service

Pensacola, FL* 1828 (purchased only) 1600 acres	Live Oak	Gulf Islands National Seashore, 1971 135,458 acres	National Park Service

*These tracks became the Naval Live Oak Plantation at Deer Point in January 1829

@Fillmore added 3,003 acres in 1853. Pierce added 3,381 acres in 1853 and 10,792 acres in 1855

^Fillmore deleted these reservations in 1853

Andrew Jackson

Original Reservation	Tree Type	Current Reservation	Authority
Santa Rosa Peninsula, FL* 1830 1216.36 acres	Live Oak, White Oak, Red Cedar	Gulf Islands National Seashore, 1971 135,458 acres	National Park Service
Steinhatchee River, FL 1832 13,376 acres	Live Oak	Steinhatchee Springs Wildlife Management Area 21,000 acres	Florida Fish and Wildlife Conservation Commission
Lakes Verret, Grass, and Palourde, LA 1832 46,838 acres#	Live Oak	Elm Hall Wildlife Management Area, 1998, 2839 acres Atchafalaya National Heritage Area, 2006 800,000 acres Live Oak Society 1934, 9000+ trees	Louisiana Department of Wildlife and Fisheries National Park Service Louisiana Garden Club

	Tree Type	Current Reservation	Authority
			Federation, Inc.
Pascagoula Bay, MS 1832 1966.59 acres	Live Oak	Mississippi National Heritage Area, 2009	Mississippi Department of Marine Resources
Mobile County, AL 1832 200 acres	Live Oak	none	Sold publically
Santa Rosa Peninsula, FL 1833 9360 acres	Live Oak	Gulf Islands National Seashore, 1971 135,458 acres	National Park Service
Choctawhatchie Bay, FL 1834 19,790 acres	Live Oak	Live Oak Point Peninsula 1000 acres	Northwest Florida Water Management District (remainder is residential)
St. Andrews Bay, FL 1834 46,251 acres	Live oak	Oaks by the Bay 5 acres	City of Panama City (remainder is residential)

#Tyler deleted these reservations in 1843, but Polk reinstated 14,720 acres in 1845

Martin Van Buren

Original Reservation	Tree Type	Current Reservation	Authority

Santa Rosa Peninsula, FL* 1838 3410 acres	Live Oak	Gulf Islands National Seashore, 1971 135,458 acres	National Park Service

James K. Polk

Original Reservation	Tree Type	Current Reservation	Authority
Grass lake, Lake Poulard, Lake Verret, Grand River, LA 1845, 14,720 acres	Live Oak	Elm Hall Wildlife Management Area, 1998, 2839 acres Atchafalaya National Heritage Area, 2006 800,000 acres Live Oak Society 1934, 9000+ trees	Louisiana Departme nt of Wildlife and Fisheries National Park Service Louisiana Garden Club Federation , Inc.

Millard Fillmore

Original Reservation	Tree Type	Current Reservation	Authority
Hillsboro River and Lake Augusta, FL 1853, 3,003 acres	Live Oak	Hillsborough River State Park, 1938 2990 acres	Florida Department of Environmen tal Protection

Franklin Pierce

Original Reservation	Tree Type	Current Reservation	Authority
East Florida 1853 14,173acres	Live Oak	Lake Runnymede Conservation Area 2007, 43 acres Split Oak Forest Wildlife and Environmental Area 1990s, 2000 acres	Osceola County Florida Fish and Wildlife Conservation Commission

James Buchanan

Original Reservation	Tree Type	Current Reservation	Authority
Suwannee River, FL 1857/1858/1859, 68,674 acres	Yellow Pine	Small preserved areas along the river	Florida Department of Environmental Protection
East Florida 1857/1858/1860 14,682 acres	Yellow Pine	Pine Island Conservation Area 880 acres	Brevard County Board of County Commissioners
Sweet Water and Black Water Rivers, FL 1857, 4482 acres	Live Oak	none	residential

There has likely been no further reaching legacy of a U.S. President that has sprung from the pure care and interest of the individual for an object or being than JQA's love of trees and gardens. This love influenced landscape architecture, environmental conservation, national policy, the celebration of national treasures and natural resources, and the caring activities of generations in the nurturing and enjoyment   of trees, flowers, crops, and other plant life. In his wide ranging efforts to establish permanent domestic and international conservation and use of botanic resources, his methods may not have had the results he specifically envisioned, but they certainly succeeded in providing level of protection for, and a plethora of enjoyment of, trees and gardens "for future generations."

For Future Generations

146

Appendix A: John Quincy Adams Timeline of Trees and Gardens

1761: John Adams inherited the saltbox house where JQA was born

July 11, 1767: Born in Braintree, Massachusetts

June 17, 1775: Witnessed the Battle of Bunker's Hill while holding his mother Abigail Adams's hand, watching from a hill near the family homestead

February 17, 1778: Sailed to Europe with his father aboard the frigate *Boston*

August 1779: Returned from Europe after his father received no diplomatic instructions

November 1779: Sailed back to Europe with his father and younger brother Charles, this time staying for seven years

December 1779: Wrote his first diary entry pertaining to gardens during the overland trip from Spain to France after landing

August 9, 1780: Toured the Physick Garden in Leiden, Holland for the first time

August 20, 1780: Toured the gardens at the country seat of Daniel Crommelin

July 7, 1781: Began the journey to St. Petersburg, Russia, as Francis Dana's secretary

May 15, 1782: Took his first tour of the Summer Garden at Peterhof

June 23, 1782: Took his first tour of the Jardin de Narischkin

Summer 1783: Reunited with his family in Auteil, France, and toured the gardens of Domaine de Chantilly

April 21, 1785: Toured the gardens at the estate of Louis de Noailles, grandfather of the Marquis de Lafayette

1785-1790: Returned to the U.S. and earned bachelor's and master's degrees at Harvard University, during which he toured local gardens

1787: John and Abigail Adams purchased Peacefield (The Old House) in Quincy

November 6, 1794: Appointed U. S. Minister to the Netherlands by George Washington until June 20, 1797

Spring 1795: While in the Netherlands, toured the gardens at the estates of the Willink brothers, and took regular walks in the woods near his lodgings in Amsterdam

February 7, 1796:   While in England during the winter of 1795/1796, accepted Louisa Johnson's friendship ring

July 1797:   Married Louisa Catherine Johnson in All-Hallows-By-The-Tower Anglican Church in London

December 5, 1797: Appointed U. S. Minister to Prussia by his father, John Adams, until May 5, 1801, during which he toured the major gardens of the region

September 1801:   Returned to the United States from Europe

September 14, 1801: On his way home to Quincy, toured the Mount Vernon Garden (now the New York Botanical Garden) and Town Hall Garden in New York City

November 4, 1801: Toured the gardens of Rose Hill Manor in Frederick, Maryland, the home of Louisa's uncle, Thomas Johnson

April 1, 1802: Elected Massachusetts State Senator until March 4, 1803

March 4, 1803: Elected U. S. Senator from Massachusetts until June 8, 1808

September 1803: As a member of the Boston Academy of Arts and Sciences, began his interest in applied botanical pursuits when fellow members encouraged him to study the *Flora Batava* journal of Dutch botanist Jan Kops. He also made his first plantings of peach stones

April 18, 1804: Laid out his first orchard of 102 apple trees on Mount Wollaston, and worked in his garden at the house of his birth all summer

April 1805: Laid out his first tree nursery for planting seeds, stones, and acorns

May 1806: Appointed Professor of Rhetoric and Oratory at Harvard University

November 5, 1809: Appointed U. S. Minister to Russia by James Madison until April 28, 1814, during which he toured the major gardens of St. Petersburg

April 1814: Appointed lead negotiator for the Treaty of Ghent by James Madison, which ended the War of 1812. During the trip from St. Petersburg to Ghent, he toured the gardens of Catherinendal in Estonia, and La Grange, home of the Marquis de Lafayette, outside of Paris

June 8, 1815: Appointed U. S. Minister to the Court of St. James (United Kingdom) by James Madison until May 14, 1817
1816: The Columbian Institute for the Promotion of Arts and Sciences was established

September 22, 1817: Appointed Secretary of State under President James Monroe until March 4, 1825

April 27, 1818: Elected to the American Philosophical Society

October 1818: Toured the Hudson River Valley, centered on Fishkill, New York, and Cedar Grove, home of nephew Peter De Wint

March 12, 1819: Supported surgeon and botanist Dr. William Barton in repairing his career, who eventually became the first Navy Surgeon General and Professor of Botany at the University of Pennsylvania, among other noted positions

June 1819: Received the latest surveys of live oak trees by James Leander Cathcart, the Navy's timber protection agent, which began his interest in preserving live oaks

December 1820: Attended his first meeting of the Columbian Institute for the Promotion of Arts and Sciences after being a member for three years

November 6, 1921: Reviewed the plans for the Columbian Institute's botanic garden by Dr. William Thornton

October 4, 1822: Elected President of the Columbian Institute

September 23, 1823: Toured the gardens of Nathaniel Amory of Watertown, Massachusetts

August 2, 1824: Toured the exotic gardens of William Yeates in Alexandria, DC

October 1, 1824: Toured the gardens of Point Breeze, home of Joseph Bonaparte, in Bordentown, New Jersey

October 3, 1824: Observed a chestnut tree planted by George Washington at Belmont Mansion, home of Judge Richard Peters, outside Philadelphia, Pennsylvania

February 9, 1825:   Elected 6th President of the United States until March 4, 1829, upon which he resigned as President   of the Columbian Institute

1826:   Had tree surveys completed of South Carolina, Georgia, and Florida live oaks

July 5, 1826: First proposed establishing a tree nursery on the White House grounds

July 18, 1826: Toured the orchard of Boston publisher Thomas Greenleaf

November 1, 1826: Made the first plantings in the White House garden of chestnuts and shellbark acorns

March 3, 1827: Signed into law "An Act for the Gradual Improvement of the Navy of the United States," which included the preservation of southern live oak forests, and approved the reservation of 3,602.25 acres of red cedar trees in Monroe County, Alabama

August 7, 1827: Began using the summer house cellar at The Old House (Peacefield) in Quincy for experimental plantations

September 10, 1827: Staked out and fenced in a tree nursery at The Old House, making the first plantings on October 3rd

September 1827: Toured the gardens of Peter Chardon Brooks, Henry Dearborn, and Israel Thorndike, as well as the Harvard University Botanic Garden

November 8, 1827: Finished preparations of the White House nursery and made the first plantings, including chestnuts, shagbarks, and black walnuts

December 1827: The circular letters and procedures to U.S. consuls were sent to collect foreign plants and seeds for the U.S. Government and the Columbian Institute, which established their botanic garden after the first deliveries arrived

December 10, 1827: Recommended a seal for the Columbian Institute which was rejected by the members on February 1828

March 1828: Samuel Southard purchased a total of 3,650 acres of live oaks in western Florida, after presenting the plan to JQA in January, who could not make the time to approve of a formal reservation of the land before his presidency ended

May 28, 1828: Illinois Senator Sidney Breese presented JQA with a petrified pear from Monroe County

August 1828: Visited Prince's Garden on Long Island, New York

January 18, 1829: The Deer Point Live Oak Reservation became the first operating federal tree farm in the U.S.

Marc 1829: Signed the bill which laid the foundation for naval reservations of live oak and others trees from 1829 to 1861 and beyond

July 17, 1829: Visited the gardens of Thomas Greenleaf, observing many exotic trees

July 18, 1829: Toured the gardens of Edward Brooks in Medford, Massachusetts

September 4, 1829: Toured the gardens of Peter Chardon Brooks

1830-1857: Presidents Andrew Jackson through James Buchanan made 15 reservations of southern live oak, yellow pine, and other types of oak trees totaling over 260,000 acres, applying the bill that JQA signed before leaving office in 1829

August-November 1830: Conceptualized an orchard with son Charles, picked a spot on the south side of Mount Wollaston, had it surveyed and staked out, and began planting trees

August 6, 1830: Toured the grounds of Nathaniel Frothingham to observe his trees in Medford, Massachusetts

September 16, 1830: Toured the grounds of Daniel Greenleaf to observe his trees

October 1830: Cleared a plot of land he called "The Stony Barren," converting it to an experimental area he renamed "The Seminary"

March 4, 1831: Elected U. S. Representative from Massachusetts until February 23, 1848, through nine re-elections

July 9, 1831: Made an honorary member of the Boston Horticultural Society

May 21, 1835: Toured Bartram's Garden in Philadelphia, now the oldest public garden in North America

1836-1842: The U.S. Exploration Expedition collected the plant specimens that would greatly contribute to the baseline of the U.S. Botanical Garden

January 12, 1836: Appointed Chairman of the Joint Committee on the Smithson Bequest

July 6, 1836: Toured the grounds of Andalusia, the estate of Nicholas Biddle

September 3, 1836: Gave his son Charles the letter seal of John Adams, which incorporated a deer, pine tree, and fish

1837: The Columbian Institute ceased operations, which temporarily suspended growth and maintenance of their botanic garden

August 4, 1837: Received from his cousin Josiah Adams a cane composed of twenty-five different kinds of wood

July 7, 1838: Examined exotic plants brought to Washington by Dr. Henry Perrine, U.S. Consul to Campeche, Mexico

September 26, 1839: Visited an exhibition of the Massachusetts Horticultural Society

May-September 1841: Argued the case of the *Amistad* before the Supreme Court

September 27, 1841: Visited by botanist and horticulturist Charles Downing who dedicated his latest book to JQA

December 10, 1841: Appointed as Chairman of the second Committee on the Smithson Legacy, the plan of which was signed by President James K. Polk in 1846

December 1841: Toured the grounds and gardens of Sharon, the residence of U.S. Navy Commodore Thomas Ap Catesby Jones in Fairfax, Virginia

Fall 1842: Granted trees to the local episcopal church in Quincy, but only planted white oaks and horse chestnuts at The Old House, being there only from September to November that year

May 16, 1843: Commemorated his years of planting at Quincy by counting 100 trees on his property planted by his hand, including a 25 foot tall maple

May 26, 1843: Toured the tulip gardens in Roxbury, Massachusetts

July-August 1843: Vacationed in Niagara Falls, commenting during the trip that the foliage made New England and New York look like a Garden of Eden

August 3, 1843: Toured the elegant gardens and greenhouse of Rensselaerswyck, the mansion house of Stephen Van Rensselaer IV in Albany, New York

December 1844: Passed on the chairmanship of the Smithson Bequest Committee to Robert Dale Owen

June 3, 1845: Received and planted ten parcels of seeds, primarily vegetables and wheat, from the U.S. Commissioner of Patents Henry Ellsworth

October 18, 1845:   After sending chestnut, apple, and shagbark trees to the horticulturist Andrew Jackson Downing in appreciation of dedicating his most recent book, *The Fruits and Fruit Trees of America,* to JQA, made his last diary entry concerning gardening when the boil on his hand returned

April 10, 1846:   President James K. Polk signed the Smithsonian Institution Bill into law after more than ten years of debate

November 20, 1846: Suffered a stroke while staying at son Charles's house in Boston, recovering ad returning to Washington by February 12, 1847

February 21, 1848: Suffered a cerebral hemorrhage on the floor of the House of Representatives

February 23, 1848: Died in the House Speaker Room

1849:   The Smithsonian Castle construction was completed

1850: The U.S. Botanical Garden was established in the same place as the original Columbian Institute botanical garden

May 15, 1852: Louisa Adams died of a heart attack in Washington, DC, and was eventually laid to rest beside her husband in Quincy, Massachusetts

1861: The start of the Civil War effectively ended naval tree reservations in the southern U.S.

1971:   The National Park Service established the Gulf Island National Seashore, part of which preserved the Deer Point Naval Live Oak Reservation, which JQA originally reserved.

Appendix B: Afterward

The idea for this book actually developed from my writing of a book about JQA on an entirely different subject. As I performed my research for *Conception of Magnificence: John Quincy Adams and the Birth of American Astronomy*, I could not help noticing biological references sprouting up amongst the astronomical references that JQA made in his diaries, and within the other sources I discovered.

As I studied JQA's diary entries as a child in Europe witnessing the first hot air balloon launches, I found that his father, John Adams, and Benjamin Franklin took him on tours of the greatest gardens in France, Holland, and the surrounding area. As I read through entries describing JQA's friendship with Tsar Alexander I and their mutual interests in astronomy during his time as Ambassador to Russia, I noticed that JQA was simultaneously visiting the Stroganov Garden, Oranienbaum, and the Czarskozelo in and around St. Petersburg. While I studied JQA's presidential activities in support of astronomy, I found descriptions of his plans and appointments in support of live oaks in the southern states, and his activities in his self-developed White House garden and nursery. During searches for his activities in

Cambridge to bring the Harvard College Observatory into existence, I found that he was touring local gardens, managing his many plots of land containing tree stands and farm crops, and spending large portions of his days in his own garden, nursery, seminary, and orchard. During his congressional efforts to support creation of the Smithsonian Institution, I found that he also took day trips to various gardens in the local Washington area, both public and private. As I followed JQA along his route to Niagara Falls and his fateful meetings with astronomer Ormsby Mitchel, moving him toward his support of the Cincinnati Observatory, I felt like I was looking over his shoulder as he observed the trees, flowers, and crops along his route through New England, New York, and eventually Pennsylvania, Ohio, Virginia, and Maryland. As I watched the movie *Amistad* for the second time, I became more aware of the scene depicting JQA working in his greenhouse, and suspected there was more meaning in that depiction as part of the story than I had previously realized.

The preponderance of arboriculture and horticulture evidence that revealed itself while searching for astronomical evidence lead me to believe that there was another story to be uncovered. I put this idea on the back burner while I developed *Conception of Magnificence.*

Once I had the time to dig deeper into JQA's tree and garden aspirations, I began looking even more deeply into his daily diary activity, far more than I did when researching his astronomical activities. I needed to obtain a clear understanding of his daily routines, the ways in which he developed his plantings techniques and experiments, and the feelings he expressed from day to day. I accompanied him on virtually every day of his life from his first serious plantings in the first few years of the 19th century until his last entry concerning trees and gardens just a few months before his death. I also learned how much his plantations created stronger and more meaningful bonds with his family, including his parents, siblings, wife, children, and grandchildren. It was an enlightening and enriching experience for me to be, if not literally, at least literately with JQA as he grew and cared for his own trees, plants, and flowers, witnessed the greatest gardens in the western world, and greatly influenced tree conservation in a great portion of the 19th century.

My growing experience with JQA's exploits with trees and gardens enhanced my interest and appreciation of my own trees and gardens. It already existed, but JQA inspired me to grow more varied types of trees, shrubs, and flowers, being more diligent in keeping them healthy and thriving, and slowing down to take my own tours to enjoy them.

It turned out that there was a story, which was far reaching in geography, vocation, and time. It could be considered as epic in its scope, but intimate in its subject matter; the relationship between a grower and his plants.

For Future Generations

162

Appendix C: Bibliography

Adams, Charles Francis, editor, *Memoirs of John Quincy Adams, comprising portions of his diary from 1795 to 1848*, Lippincott, Philadelphia, 1874-77

Adams, William R., "Florida Live Oak Farm of John Quincy Adams," *The Florida Historical Quarterly*, Vol. 51 No. 2, Florida Historical Society, Cocoa, Florida, October 1972

Massachusetts Historical Society, *The Adams Papers Digital Edition*, Massachusetts Historical Society Internet Website

Massachusetts Historical Society, *The Diaries of John Quincy Adams, A Digital Collection*, Massachusetts Historical Society Internet Website

Massachusetts Historical Society, *The John Quincy Adams Digital Diary*, Massachusetts Historical Society Internet Website

McEwan, Barbara, *White House Landscapes: Horticultural Achievements of American Presidents*, Walker, New York, 1992

McKindley, Mona Rose, *With a Heart of Oak: John Quincy Adams, Scientific Farmer and Landscape Gardener*, Harvard University, Cambridge, 2013

National Park Service, *Cultural Landscape Inventory, Peace Field, Adams National Historic Park*, Denver Service Center, 2012

Snell, Charles W., *Special History Study: A History of the Naval Live Oak History Program, 1794-1880: A Forgotten Chapter in the History of American Conservation*, Denver Service Center, National Park Service, September 1983

Solit, Karen D., *History of the United States Botanic Garden 1816-1891*, Architect of the Capitol, Washington, 1993

Todisco, Patrice, "Peacefield," Landscape Notes Internet Website, June 1, 2015

Appendix D: Index